TRIPLE OVERTIME

Coach John Grussendorf

Triple Overtime, © 1986, John A. Grussendorf
All rights reserved.
Printed in the U.S.A.

DEDICATION

We lovingly dedicate this book to . . . the hundreds of people who have upheld us in prayer. May it be to the glory of God and a blessing to many.
John and Mary Grussendorf
with our daughters
Miranda
Angela
Brenda
Tanya

"*Praise be to the God and Father of our Lord Jesus Christ, the Father of compassion and God of all comfort, who comforts us in all our troubles so that we can comfort those in any trouble with the comfort we ourselves have received from God.*"
II Corinthians 1:3,4
New International Version

ACKNOWLEDGEMENTS

We sincerely wish to thank all those who have shared in telling "our story" — the doctors for their medical information and comments, the basketball coaches for their recollections, the thoughts by the basketball girls, the pastors, friends and family. We deeply appreciate your contributions which we know will be of great interest to the reader.

Special love and thanks also to my wonderful mother-in-law, Helen Aili, who played a very vital part in helping us prepare and compile this book.

THE GRUSSENDORFS

CONTENTS

PREFACE: Mary Grussendorf

FAMILY HISTORY OF JOHN

CHAPTER I: The Montana Adventure

CHAPTER II: Back in Esko

CHAPTER III: First Overtime

CHAPTER IV: Second Overtime

CHAPTER V: Graft vs. Host Disease

CHAPTER VI: Third Overtime

CHAPTER VII: The Sharing of "OUR STORY"

GLOSSARY OF MEDICAL TERMS

PREFACE

"But those who hope in the LORD will renew their strength. They will soar on wings like eagles; they shall run and not grow weary, they will walk and not be faint." Isaiah 40:31

I am honored to be able to share in "John's Story". Together, with our family and a host of friends, we have experienced, in part, the depths of suffering and pain — and then the heights of joy and happiness as we have witnessed the healing power of God through prayer.

It has been very hard to see my husband go through so much sickness and suffering. Words really can't even begin to express the hurt and ache in my heart for John, along with my own fear of losing him and being left alone to raise our four daughters. Life at times seemed almost unbearable! But Christ in His infinite love lifted us above these struggles and trials and drew us closer to Him and to one another. We, as a family, have learned to treasure and share every moment. Thank you, Jesus, for taking care of us so dearly!

In spite of our adversities, we can be an inspiration!! *John has proved this to be true.* He is so thankful just to be alive. He lives his life to the fullest each day, putting many of us to shame with his vigor and enthusiasm! Life itself has taken on a different meaning and he has learned to enjoy the simple things. As he says, "we must take time to smell the roses".

Behind the medical victories are the struggles of courage and faith by a man "tried in the furnace of affliction" — who, through it all, gives praise to God for His great love and mercy. May his story touch our hearts as we join him in praise.

"See, I have refined you, though not as silver; I have tested you in the furnace of affliction."
Isaiah 48:10

Mary

FAMILY HISTORY OF JOHN

John Allen Grussendorf was born in Duluth, Minnesota, on September 8, 1945, to Mr. and Mrs. Diedrich Grussendorf, who now reside in Hermantown, Minnesota. He has an older sister Eleanor (Ellie) Puumala of Minneapolis, two older brothers Jim and Carl and a younger brother Tom, all of Hermantown, Minnesota.

His father (Deke) had taught school at Two Harbors High School and the Grand Rapids Agricultural School. Later he became an Agricultural Agent for the St. Louis County of Northeastern Minnesota and afterwards established the Grussendorf Nursery, a business which is still owned and operated by the family. It was only natural that all the boys have learned the art of landscaping and work well as a "team".

Soon after completing his college education at UMD, John married Mary Aili (the daughter of the late Rev. Waino and Helen Aili of Esko, Minnesota) on June 15, 1968. In August of 1970, they purchased a hobby farm in rural Esko and are still living there. They have been blessed with four daughters— Miranda, Angela, Brenda and Tanya.

John coached boys basketball for ten years, first at Mellen, Wisconsin during 1968-69 and later at Toivola-Meadowlands, Clover Valley and the Albrook Schools; working at the family nursery during the summer months. For the last five years he has been Head Coach of the Girls Basketball team in Esko.

Chapter 1

The Montana Adventure

On a vacation trip out west in 1979, we fell in love with the beauty of the Bitterroot Valley in Montana. We thought maybe someday we'd like to live there. Our dream came true the following year in March of 1980. I took a two year leave of absence from our family owned Grussendorf Nursery of Duluth, Minnesota, to venture out on a landscaping business of my own in the Bitterroot Valley. Our destination — Hamilton, Montana — located 44 miles south of Missoula.

We rented our 60 acre farm in Esko, Minnesota to John and Sue Foley. We had no worries leaving things in their care. They proved to be excellent renters. Our neighbors and close friends, John and Marie Bonneville with their two sons, were to be the landlords and also in charge of the beef cattle we owned in partnership.

On our arrival in Hamilton, we first rented a mobile home from Melvin and Darlene Kraft. Our girls attended the Darby Elementary School with Miranda in the fourth grade, Angela in the third, Brenda in the second and Tanya in kindergarten.

After visiting various churches in the valley, we decided to attend Christ's Bible Church served by Pastor William Springstead. We immediately felt at home in the fellowship there. At the end of May, we moved and rented a two bedroom furnished cottage from our Sunday School teachers, Bill and Marie Piatt. They owned a lovely ranch at the base of the Bitterroot Mountains.

All during this time I was busy working for Ken Wanner at the Bitterroot Nursery and doing my own landscaping in the afternoons. Soon Mary, the girls and I had our own business going. It was a lot of hard work and long hours but we enjoyed our new environment. Even the girls pitched in to water the shrubs and spread the decorative rock.

I hadn't been feeling totally up to par before our move. We thought the diarrhea I was experiencing since January was due to the excitement and pressure of the move itself along with the establishing of our new business. Our family doctor back home was contacted and he thought things would change after we relaxed and settled in. However, he suggested checking our drinking water and taking a stool sample to the hospital to be analyzed. These revealed nothing. I kept feeling tired, losing weight and having diarrhea. Therefore, we went to see a specialist, Dr. Cain, in Missoula. He did a colonoscopy and various tests and found out that I had ulcerative colitis. This was in July of 1980. The prescribed medication seemed to help somewhat and we kept busy throughout the summer with our landscaping business. However, there were times when I'd have to hurry into someone's home and ask to use their bathroom —a truly humiliating request. One item I always carried with me was an extra pair of underwear. Some of our friends noticed that I wasn't feeling well even though I tried to put on a good appearance.

In spite of it all, we enjoyed the summer —sightseeing, picnics, fishing and swimming in the Bitterroot River. Another memorable event was the erupting of Mt. St. Helen's on May 18th. The volcanic ash drifted 1,000 miles to us in Hamilton. Schools were closed and ash had to be swept off the cars and sidewalks. We played on the church softball team and often had get-togethers with Craig and Evie Ekin and other church friends. Cy Morrison, Evie's grandpa, took the girls under his wing and treated them like his own granddaughters. That love bond still remains today. Miranda, our oldest, at 11½ years had an exciting experience. She was able to go on a "pack trip" through the Bitterroot Mountains into Idaho riding a horse! She was in good hands with our trusted landlord, Bill Piatt, his son Kevin, and Lindy Ash. She owes the joy of that experience to them and I know she will forever be grateful.

The girls were now attending the Corvallis School, getting on the bus each morning with senior, Tami Piatt. They had gotten to love her as an older sister and felt confident going to a strange school with her as chaperone.

As summer was drawing to a close, Craig and six others began to plan a deer hunting trip. I had been eagerly looking forward to this adventure and to use my "long bow". It would've been most enjoyable had I not felt sick the whole time. With six people in a tepee, it was most embarrassing to get up many times a night because of the diarrhea. I came home tired and worn out! Bill Piatt commented that "he knew something was wrong."

At the end of August, without mentioning anything to the rest of the family, Mary had started praying that the Lord would give direction for our lives —whether to remain in Hamilton or go back to Minnesota. In a few short days the answer came. Two factors led to our decision to move back. First, it was the matter of my health and the second was a letter I received from Mr. Bob Swanstrom, the sixth grade teacher in Esko. He informed me that the head girls basketball coaching position was open — would I be interested? He would be the assistant. We discussed the matter with Bill and Marie Piatt and we all came to the conclusion that it was the Lord's leading.

Thus, our Montana dream came to an end. We had lived there seven months. It was a wonderful experience and we made many lasting friendships. We hope someday to make a trip back to see them and also the growth of our landscaping.

Mary's mother, who we call "Gram", and her brother Phil, flew out in October and stayed a few days. They had come to help drive one of our vehicles back to Minnesota. After our sad farewells to all our friends in Hamilton, Gram and Phil headed out to Esko driving the Nursery truck, towing our extra car. We, as a family, headed to the Mayo Clinic in Rochester, Minnesota. There we met with Dr. McPherson who had been recommended to us by the doctor in Missoula. The diagnosis was the same — ulcerative colitis.

Chapter II

Back In Esko

Until now I had always coached boys basketball teams. If someone had told me that I would really enjoy coaching the girls, I would have laughed. I have since found it to be a tremendously challenging experience. I have found out that girl athletes will take more discipline and punishment than boys. Maybe it's because they want to prove to me that they can take anything I dish out to them — and boy did I dish it out!!!

The basketball season in Esko began in November of 1980. It was my first year together with Bob Swanstrom as the Assistant Coach. He was an excellent partner and very well organized. I was anxious and excitedly looking forward to the season but always there was the reminder of my colitis problem. This made my first year of coaching physically very hard. During games, the first thing I would look for on entering a school was the restroom in case a quick exit was necessary. Always I carried a change of underwear!! I had informed the Assistant Coach to take over as if nothing was wrong. That year was a humbling as well as a rewarding experience for me as a coach and as a friend to my ballplayers. We had a good season and Bob proved to be a great assistant in many ways. All this time I had been on medication for the colitis but it hadn't helped much.

In April of 1981, the nursery work began as usual. I lived through pure torture that whole summer. More than once while driving the truck, I would have to pull over and head for the woods — again with the extra underwear handy! Many times I would cry aloud and ask the Lord to take away this affliction — but I guess He had other plans! At home, the girls were always on the alert. If they heard Dad coming when they were in the bathroom, they would have to scoot down to the bathroom in the basement. This was a natural! Pretty soon Dad had total priority! The tension and pressure of the situation was getting unbearable.

In July of 1981 after having a lower GI and x-rays, Dr. Puumala in Cloquet, Minnesota, again confirmed "ulcerative colitis". The prescribed treatment didn't bring much relief and I wasn't able to endure much more of this. The situation was hard on Mary and the girls too. They wondered when would Dad get better? Something had to be done!

My sister-in-law, Sandie Grussendorf, knew of a friend from nurses' training who had worked with colon specialists. I visited her and received names and information which helped us get an appointment in Minneapolis with the Colon and Rectal Associates. This was in September of 1981. Mary and I met with Dr. Frederic Nemer—a wonderful doctor. He put us at ease with a thorough explanation and he took time to answer all our questions. After a colonoscopy, we found out that my whole large intestine was affected.

Following the initial examination, he explained to us about the "Park's Pouch". He felt I was a good candidate for this. We went home to study the literature. There were only a small number who had undergone this procedure. It would involve an eight to ten hour surgery. I would also have a temporary ileostomy for approximately three months while the pouch would heal.

Proctocolectomy with ileal reservoir and anal anastomosis

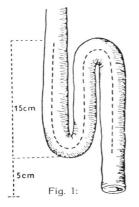

Fig. 1:
Alignment of small bowel loops.

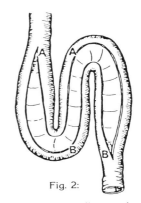

Fig. 2:
Antimesenteric wall opened.

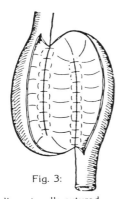

Fig. 3:
Adjacent walls sutured.

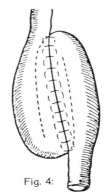

Fig. 4:
Reservoir completed.

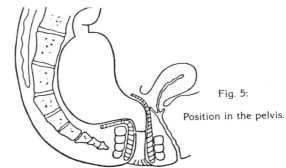

Fig. 5:
Position in the pelvis.

During this interim, the second basketball season had begun (1981-1982). As we pondered this medical decision, I felt that, without question, I could leave Bob in charge of the team and if all went well I could be back after Christmas vacation.

After much discussion and prayer, we felt that we really had no alternative. The surgery was scheduled for December 14, 1981. Gram came to stay with the girls. Sister Ellie, Mother and Dad were with Mary and me at the hospital. We embraced, had our private talk and cried in each others arms just before going into surgery. Naturally, we all were fearful but we put our trust in the Lord. We knew that God was in control of everything and we were uplifted knowing that many were praying in our behalf!

By Mary

"The family members and I went to the surgical waiting room. Throughout the 10 hour surgery we were kept informed. The attendants in the waiting room would receive a call and relay the message to us. The first was that John was asleep and things were going to begin. Next came the message that the colon or large intestine had been completely removed and construction of the pouch was about to begin. Next we heard that they were finishing up and that John would be brought to the recovery room. We were so thankful for these messages from Dr. Nemer. He personally came later to tell us that everything went fine. John was brought back to his room with 8 different tubes coming out of his body. He didn't have to go to the intensive care as this floor was equipped and staffed for these cases."

After the surgery I was in terrible pain with an incision from below the navel to the rib cage. Dr. Nemer had instructed the nurses that I be given hypos on demand. The usual is every 4 hours but I would need them every ½ to 1 hour sometimes. The nose tube I had was almost unbearable. It irritated my throat so that I could not even swallow to ease the pain. Dr. Nemer assured Mary and me that all was under control and after about a week my intestines started functioning. The nose tube was taken out and the catheter removed. We praised God that progress was being made. A special ostomy nurse schooled us on the care of the ileostomy and after 10 days we were on our way home to Esko. Oh how good it was to see our children and get back to coaching girls basketball.

Chapter III

The First Overtime

Why, why? I am sure we all have had occasion to ask why? Why all the suffering, sickness and human tragedies? Why are some healed instantly and others take long periods of time? Some are "taken" despite our deepest prayers — and many seem to have more than their share of suffering and disappointment! We are bound to have moments of doubt and despair as we question God's purposes. One thing is sure, we must all stand in awe of His wisdom and power. He uses many different means to draw our attention to Himself. Our greatest comfort comes from totally surrendering all questionings to Almighty God and *in faith accepting His will.* These are mysteries we don't understand and we can only exclaim — "O, the depth of the riches of the wisdom and knowledge of God! How unsearchable His judgments and His paths beyond tracing out!" Romans 11:33

For the remainder of the coaching year until March of 1982, I lived with a temporary ileostomy. It had its problems, but all in all we thank the Lord that things went as smoothly as they did. It was just amazing to think that I had missed only one game and that game was during Christmas vacation. I coached the rest of the season by faith, will power, guts and much prayer!

Dr. Nemer had given me pain pills and they would help me through each game. The girls had responded well and we had a successful season. Eventually we lost in the District Semi-Finals.

On March 7th, I went back to Abbott Northwestern Hospital for my ileostomy take down and the hook-up to the Parks' Pouch. The operation went so well that Dr. Nemer felt he could leave town and flew to Kentucky to attend a conference. Mary had been with me constantly but she too had left to be home overnight and was returning the next day to take me back.

Then it happened!!! One day before I was to go home I started to bleed internally! I bled from my nose and rectum — large amounts of coagulated blood. The nurses tried to keep me comfortable. My sister Eleanore, a nurse who lives in the Twin Cities, was by my side all day. About 4 or 5 o'clock in the afternoon I cried to her and asked her to tell Mary and the girls, Mom and Dad and my brothers that I loved them and to forgive me if I had offended them in anyway. I truly believed I was going to die. Then it happened — I stopped breathing! I had gone into respiratory arrest!!

Ellie had gone to the nurses' station a bit earlier and she noticed this machine being brought into my room (used to revive people who had stopped breathing) and she ran after it saying to herself — "he meant it — he knew he was going to die!" But — the Lord Jesus Christ had other plans for my life! During this emergency operation, I went through 49 units of blood as they were trying to find out where the bleeding was coming from. Now 49 units of blood during an operation is just about unheard of!! When the doctors opened me up, my body cavity was filled with coagulated blood — all around my intestines, kidneys and liver. Dr. Goldberg took my intestines in his hands and milked them of the blood that was in them. They cleaned out my cavity as best they could and sewed me back up. They could not find — and never *did* find out where I was bleeding from! Do you want to know why dear friends? — because Jesus Christ stopped the bleeding!! He healed my insides!! The bleeding had stopped while they were working on me. Hundreds of people who had been notified were praying for me and the bleeding stopped!!!

My wife, Mary, didn't get to the hospital in time to see me before I went into surgery. She was completely overwhelmed when she arrived with my sisters-in-law, Bette and Sandie, to be told that I was in emergency surgery. Oh how hard it must have been for my dear beloved wife Mary! I love her so! Next to the Lord — she has been and is my strength through it all!

I woke up in the Intensive Care and there I stayed for 4 or 5 days in terrible and constant pain. The same incision had been reopened that just 5 days before had been used to connect the pouch to my intestine. The pain was so bad—not only in the stomach area but the nose tube was unbearable — creating another terrible sore throat. Dr. Nemer (back from his trip) had again ordered hypos on demand. I was getting shots not only in my rear but also my thighs and through IV. My bottom was like an overused pin cushion! This is when Mary became alarmed because I started hallucinating. She would go out into the hallway and cry. If the shots, at best, took away some of the pain, I wanted them. I guess Dr. Nemer knew how much I could take and he reassured Mary that everything was under control. I would "see" semi-trucks driving along the "curtain tracks" — going by a farm house and finally driving into a ditch. Or I would see my mother sweeping out my room — of course, it was the cleaning lady — and I'd be seeing and talking to people who weren't there. I understand now how easily people can get "hooked" on drugs. They take the pain away — they take your senses away — it was scary to say the least!

After the bleeding, I had lost 20 pounds. I was down to 147 pounds. I looked like I had been in a concentration camp. I didn't look good but I was alive!! Slowly I began to improve and after 5 days, I was transferred to a regular room where I stayed for 2 or 3 days. Finally, the happy day arrived and we went home to our farm in Esko. I was so anxious to see my girls! I love my family so much — I didn't want to leave them yet!

I would like at this time to acknowledge again my sincere appreciation to Julian Bertogliat, the Esko Athletic Director, and to Bob Swanstrom for their great labor of love in getting blood donors for me — and I also want to thank each individual who helped out in this way. It is humbling to know there are so many friends who truly cared. May God bless you all!

By Gram:

I remember how deeply John was touched by the words of the song I quoted on a card to him shortly after his experience with the bleeding.

"When peace like a river attendeth my way,
When sorrows like sea billows roll;
Whatever my lot, Thou hast taught me to say,
It is well, it is well with my soul.

Though Satan should buffet, though trials
  should come,
Let this blest assurance control,
That Christ hath regarded my helpless estate,
And hath shed His own blood for my soul.

He lives, O the bliss of this glorious thought;
My sin, not in part, but the whole,
Is nailed to the cross and I bear it no more,
Praise the Lord, Praise the Lord, O my soul.

And, Lord haste the day when our faith
  shall be sight,
The clouds be rolled back as a scroll,

The trumpet shall sound and the Lord
  shall descend;
Even so — it is well with my soul"

H.C. Spafford 1876
Phillip Paul Bliss 1876

How wonderful to have the peace and assurance that all is well and to give yourself totally into His will!

According to Ecclesiastes 3:1-18 "There is a time for everything, and a season for every activity under heaven: A time to be born and a time to die — etc." It is at times like these, when you face a matter of life and death, that it is so good to "know in whom you have believed" — to know that things are right between you and your God.

Chapter IV

The Second Overtime

Nursery work was just 2 to 3 weeks away and I asked the Lord to give me the strength to be able to meet the first day with my brothers and to help in any way I could. He answered this prayer and I was at work — weak, but there. Praise the Lord!! April and May went. June and July came and went! I was working but not feeling as strong as I thought I should. I gained back the 20 pounds but I still wasn't feeling the best. The Park's Pouch or Ileal-Anal Reservoir was working alright. I could control my bowel movements.

When I had undergone the emergency operation in March which required 49 units of blood, Dr. Fromke, the blood specialist at Abbott Northwestern Hospital, had requested that I come back in August for some routine blood work. My appointment was for August — so Mary and I went, thanking the Lord for delivering me from the death bed. The blood technician took a few vials of blood and sent me on my way.

Two days later the doctor called and informed me to come to Minneapolis as soon as possible — the blood tests had shown some abnormalities! Some abnormality! — no wonder I didn't feel as strong as I should have the past summer. Normal hemoglobin for an adult male is 12 or 13 — mine was 8 - 9. Hemoglobin is an indicator of your strength or stamina. Platelets normal for an adult male are anywhere from 140,000 to 400,000. Mine came in at a low 6,000. The medical people wondered why I wasn't bleeding to death inside. This is extremely low! What do platelets do? They coagulate the blood so the coagulation strength of my blood was very dangerously low. During the month of August, I had experienced a little bleeding in my stool but I didn't think much of it.

The normal white blood cell count for an adult is 4,000 to 10,000. I believe mine was riding at 2,000 to 2,500. What do these cells do? They help fight disease and germs as they enter your body. So, from these reports we knew there was trouble but they didn't know what it was until they took a bone marrow test. This is a test where bone marrow from your hip is extracted with a hollow needle as you lay on your stomach. I may be a big baby — but the pain was terrible for about 5 seconds. I just about squeezed my wife's hand off as they did this procedure. I believe it took a day or so to get the results so Mary and I had plenty of time to discuss and collect our thoughts. We prayed desperately that it wouldn't be anything serious — hoping that some medication would take care of it all and we would be on our way home to be with the "kids" again!

Well, the Lord answered our prayers but not in the way we wanted Him to. We, as Christians, must realize that prayers aren't always answered according to our desires. It is His will, not ours — His will be done!! Sometimes this is hard to understand and we question why? Why? Why? This is when our faith is tested and ours was to be deeply tested during the next year or so!

Finally, the blood doctor came to visit us in our room. My sister, Ellie, Mary and I were sitting and visiting when he came in. His countenance immediately told us the news wasn't good. He sat down and his first words were — "John, I don't have good news — your bone marrow has shut down and we don't know the reason for this. We didn't find any form of cancer but we believe you have a disease called Aplastic Anemia. This means your bone marrow has shut down for no apparent reason and is not producing any cells of any kind. This is why your hemoglobin, platelets and white blood cell counts are way down". It was just a matter of days or weeks that if the blood counts were down I would either bleed to death inside or catch a cold, sore throat or pneumonia and die because of the lack of blood cells to fight the infection.

Mary and I cried as the doctor tried to explain what I had — but at that time we couldn't listen. We were too distraught and emotionally upset. This is where my faith was tested and I have to say my faith wavered. All I could think of is, why me? I had just gotten over one death threat — now, I was facing another one. It was definitely a low point in my life.

At this time the doctor recommended that I be transferred to the University of Minnesota Hospitals — as they are one of the pioneers in bone marrow transplant procedures. He arranged for us to be moved there that afternoon. When we arrived at the hospital we were placed on the cancer floor. This was truly devastating to Mary and me. It seemed our minds and bodies were functioning on reflexes alone and as the doctors and nurses came to visit and ask questions, we were numb with fear and apprehension. I did try to use a little humor — I asked the nurse to take Mary's blood pressure as she had her own cot in my room also but this didn't uplift our spirits.

Now comes another bone marrow test and more pain. The following days I was given blood transfusions to get my platelets up to 80,000. At this time I also received a Hickman Catheter and we received instructions on the proper care of it.

HICKMAN CATHETER

(A Hickman Catheter is an IV made of flexible plastic tube that is put into a large neck vein. The tip of it is in the right chamber of the heart. This does not interfere with your heart's normal functions, nor does it interfere with your normal activity. The end of the catheter comes out from under the skin at your chest. This end can be used to draw blood and to give transfusions, chemotherapy and nutritional supplements without puncturing your skin. It is a painless way of having frequent blood tests taken.)

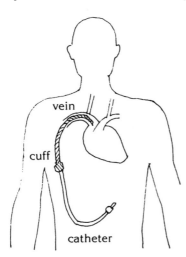

The Hickman catheter is a specially designed, soft flexible tube. It is used to provide a direct route into a large blood vessel or vein. The tip of the catheter lies within the large vein near the heart. The striped length of the catheter lies just under the skin. There is a small dacron cuff just above the site where the catheter comes out of the skin (exit-site). You can feel this cuff as a small bump under the skin. Body tissue will heal into this cuff in about 3 weeks and make it difficult (but still possible) to pull the catheter out.

The skin exit-site is the place were the catheter comes out of the body. The exit-site is a break in the skin and therefore bacteria may enter and grow. For this reason, the site must be cleansed carefully with a bacteria killing solution. The catheter exit-site should be checked daily for any signs of redness, swelling, tenderness or drainage.

Heparin is a medication that prevents blood clotting. "Heparin-lock" means that heparin is placed inside the catheter to keep blood out and to prevent clotting inside. It is one of the most important ways you can keep your catheter working properly. The heparin-lock procedure is used immediately after fluids or medications have stopped. You must heparin-lock within 3-4 minutes to prevent clotting.

This is where I would receive all my medication and blood transfusions. It proved to be a welcome blessing and spared me from all the needles! Statistics show that 4 out of 100,000 people get Aplastic Anemia. They never did find out how I contacted it. Some live day by day on transfusions, some receive a bone marrow transplant and others die because there is no suitable donor.

The doctor wanted blood samples from my Father, Mother, sister Ellie and my three brothers, Jim, Carl and Tom. After 2 to 3 days it was found that brother Tom's blood make-up was the closest to mine. I was so thankful to have a donor. There are people who have many family members but are unable to find a compatible donor or the situation where one is an only child. So, you can see I had much to thank the Lord for! Yet it was frightening to think of what was ahead.

I celebrated my 37th birthday in the hospital on September 8, 1982. Ellie made two different types of cheesecake and brought them to the hospital for me. I guess my heart truly wasn't into this party. I had lots on my mind. Angela had had her 12th birthday when we were at the hospital and Miranda's 13th birthday was coming up on the 20th of September. Who knew what was ahead? — Only God!

Finally when they thought it was safe, I was sent home to wait. Wait for what? Wait for room to open up on the transplant floor. There are only 10 rooms in this unit and they were all filled at the present time. I had to be very careful not to pick up any bug during this waiting period. The times were very trying, tiring and unbelievably hard to bear! One thing for sure, it was great to see the girls. I love them so dearly and I knew that their hearts were breaking, as was mine. We all lived with underlying tension.

We called Pastor Wayne Juntunen and the elders of the church to come over to anoint me and pray over me (as instructed in Scripture; James 5:14,15) that my bone marrow would "kick in" by itself and just start working again — and if this was not in God's divine plan, that then the transplant would be successful and I would survive it! Three out of ten patients die after this kind of transplant.

The next couple of weeks were rough! During this wait I ran fevers periodically and also experienced some rectal bleeding. The brothers who all lived in the vicinity would come to visit and try to cheer me up but we were walking through a "deep valley". Mary, our girls and I lived every day in despair because of this dreadful, killing disease. But sometimes we forget that Jesus, our dear precious Saviour, has everything under control!! I thought often of the poem, "Footprints", which explains how Jesus walks beside us all the time but when times get rough and hard to bear, He *carries* us!! How true this was — as we found out as the days went by. For now, we knew that we couldn't make it without Him carrying us!! Praise God!!

Footprints

One night a man had a dream. He dreamed he was walking along the beach with the Lord. Across the sky flashed scenes from his life. For each scene, he noticed two sets of footprints in the sand; one belonging to him and the other to the LORD.

When the last scene of his life flashed

before him, he looked back at the footprints in the sand. He noticed that many times along the path of his life there was only one set of footprints. He also noticed that it happened at the very lowest and saddest times in his life.

This really bothered him and he questions the LORD about it. "LORD, you said that once I decided to follow you, you'd walk with me all the way. But I have noticed that during the most troublesome times in my life, there is only one set of footprints. I don't understand why when I needed you most you would leave me."

The Lord replied, "My precious, precious child, I love you and I would never leave you. During your times of trial and suffering, when you see only one set of footprints, it was then that I carried you."

"Author Unknown"

On Sunday morning, September 26th, I awoke with swollen and infected eyes. Mary and I went to the emergency room at the hospital in Duluth where the doctor recommended that I go to Minneapolis. He talked to Dr. Phil McGlave there and they felt that because of my low blood counts I should be admitted.

We called Gram and asked if she could come and stay with the girls. She was always so willing to help out and move in at a moments notice. We have thanked the Lord many times over for her. It was very sad and tearful saying our goodbyes knowing that we possibly would be staying for the transplant. Yet, I was glad the time had come because it was getting difficult to go on as I was. My brother Jim and his wife, Bette, brought Mary and me to Minneapolis.

This whole procedure seemed so frightening and awesome to us! We still hoped and prayed for the Lord to intervene with healing — otherwise this would be the only alternative. I had this prayer up until transplant time. I was admitted to Station 41, the Bone Marrow Unit, the following day which was Monday, September 27th. It was frightening to walk by all the closed doors to get to our room. The air is constantly being filtered in the room and all who enter *must* wash their hands thoroughly with antiseptic soap. Mary was able to stay right in the room with me. She had a portable chairbed that she slept in. I was so thankful to have her right by my side.

I felt numb as the nurse went through the regular routine questions and instructions. On Wednesday, I would begin my four days of chemotherapy treatment of cytoxan. The first day went well but I was nauseated for the next three. Thank goodness for Sunday — that was called my "Rest Day".

Now I would face the transplant. Bewildered and apprehensive, but in faith I looked to God for comfort and strength. We praised God for the hundreds who were again praying for me all *across the U.S.* — even friends in Finland. I had scribbled this Bible verse in a notebook — Deuteronomy 31:8 "And the Lord, He it is that doth go before thee; He will be with thee, He will not fail thee, neither forsake thee: fear not, neither be dismayed".

On Monday, my brother Tom, the donor, was admitted to the hospital at 10:00 a.m. Words cannot even begin to express the closeness and appreciation, but above all the *love* I have for him. He was going to give me *life*, the Lord willing! It was a very tiring day for me. I had to go for a preliminary radiation treatment where they made all the markings on my body in the correct places. My white count was sitting right where they wanted — at 50. They wanted my whole blood system knocked down so that the new marrow would take hold, prosper and multiply.

October 5, 1982 was "Transplant Day". Tom was brought to the operating room at 11:00 a.m. After anesthesia, they withdrew 750 cc of concentrated bone marrow from his hip bone area with a hollow needle. I could relate to what he was experiencing because I had had several of them previously. I went for radiation treatment at 11:30 a.m. as a final procedure to wipe out my system. It was very tough! It lasted longer than I anticipated. I had a sore back to begin with and then to lay on that hard table — I could hardly take it. I felt very sick and could not eat all day.

One super blessing I received that afternoon was that I was moved to a large room. It relieved me of the cramped feeling I had in the other room and there were several chairs and even a table. It was more noisy because of the filter running but I had extra floor space for walking around.

At 5:30 p.m. the marrow arrived. It was given to me through my Hickman Catheter. It resembled dark, thick blood. It took from 5:30 to 7:30 p.m. I was really tired and slept through most of it because of the radiation treatment and the moving. Mary and Ellie watched it go in a drop at a time. I know a lot of prayers were being said for me at this very hour. My Dad and Mom were back and forth between Tom and myself. I only needed 215 cc of the 750 cc because Tom's marrow was so loaded with cells and so concentrated. Mary went to see Tom in his room but he was sleeping. With tear-filled eyes she gave Sandie, his wife, a hug. That seemed to say it all!!

Wednesday, October 6th, was called "Day 1". Ellie brought Mary a notebook so that she could record the days and the blood counts, etc. One sign we looked for to know that the marrow was beginning to work, was a rise in the white count. Isn't it a miracle how the marrow can be injected into the vein and then it finds its way to the sternum and hip bones where it is located!

I was given MTX (methotrexate) which prevents your body from rejecting the marrow.

(I have taken the following information from Mary's journal, adding my own thoughts and feelings).

October 7—"Day 2". . . I'm trying to keep up on my push-ups and sit-ups. My white count went up to 100, although the doctors (Dr. McGlave and Dr. Rank) informed us that there usually is a false start, especially this early. I received platelets which is the clotting factor in the blood. That evening around 8:30, I got the chills and shakes and my temperature rose to 103 degrees. Then after awhile I cooled back down.

October 8—"Day 3". . . They wanted me to keep busy with little projects to do so they brought me some leather to make belts. I made 4 of them — one for each of my daughters. The same thing happened again after receiving platelets — very bad shakes and chills with my temperature up to 105 degrees.

October 9—"Day 4". . . I had a temperature of 102 all day. I stayed in bed except for getting up to eat. Mary rarely left my room except to use the washroom facilities or mail a card or letter to the girls. This time I was given some pre-medication before the platelets and all went well. My temperature at 10:00 p.m. was 99. Ellie came to visit every day, bringing goodies or more knitting yarn for Mary. She made a sweater for each of the girls and a deer latch-hook for me. I know she needed these projects to work on. Many times she had to just stand by and watch and could do nothing to help.

October 10—"Day 5". . . Every morning I left the room with a mask on to take a bath. That was the only time I got out and it got to be that I didn't even look forward to it. My digestive system was beginning to act up with these drugs, therefore causing diarrhea. The ointment wasn't helping a great deal so I had to resort to a heat lamp several times a day — another added bother!

October 11—"Day 6". . . I was beginning to have hope that I might be one of the very few who don't lose their hair to chemotherapy. But — I guess not, there was evidence in the bathtub.

October 12—"Day 7". . . Well, Mary shaved my head with the electric razor in the morning. I thought she'd cry — but didn't! I made Ellie a belt and also a rubber mat for outside her doorway at home. The doctors wanted us to keep busy and not just lay in bed. I was up all day. My Hickman Catheter had to be removed because it had become infected. It was a simple procedure and I knew I'd have another put in after a couple days. I started receiving Prednisone at midnight, 8:00 a.m. and 4:00 p.m.

October 13—"Day 8". . . This was a down right terrible day for me! I received OKT3 which suppresses my immune system. After about 10 or 15 minutes of this drug, I got the awful chills and shakes. My temperature rose in 15 minutes to 106+. It went right to the top of the thermometer. The chills and shakes just wouldn't subside. I started breathing very rapidly. I couldn't seem to catch my breath (Hyperventilating). They gave me injections into the IV of Benadryl, Hydrocortisone and finally Demerol. The shakes slowly began to lessen and I now had to start taking off some of the blankets. After breathing into a paper bag, I started to settle down. I remember Mary and Ellie praying for me out loud! Ellie, being a nurse, probably knew too much about what was happening. Many times over, Mary has said she's been glad to just be by my side and be ignorant medically. I think she would have panicked many a time!! I quieted down although I still was hot! Besides being sponged down with ice water, I also needed a cooling blanket. After the temperature came down, they started the drug again. *I had to receive it!* The whole procedure took about 4 hours and everything went okay except my temperature went back up to 105. So — it was more ice water and sponging by the nurse, Mary and Ellie. Finally, after what seemed ages, the temperature dropped. What a workout! I was tired and thoroughly exhausted.

October 14—"Day 9". . . Boy, was I scared! I had to receive the OKT3 again. They administered it in a four hour span — very slowly from 10:00 a.m. to 2:00 p.m. Praise the Lord, everything went fine. No temp at all — the highest it got was 99. The initial dose must have been the trouble maker. That evening I got hiccups which lasted about 2 days. I couldn't stop them. What a nuisance!

October 15—"Day 10". . .This was truly a day to Praise and Thank the Lord!! White blood cell count was 300. We had been anxiously waiting for this day and hoped the cell count was for real and wouldn't drop down. The doctors felt it was on the rise. I left my room from 8:30 to 9:30 in the morning to have the Hickman catheter put back in. One advantage is that all the medications are administered through it plus my blood drawn from it which saves me being "stuck" every morning. Also, I don't need an IV needle in my arm either. The side of my neck began to hurt and it seemed a nerve had been injured. Also, I'm beginning to get a sore throat and it hurts to swallow.

October 16 "Day 11". . .White blood count is *500*, Praise the Lord. I had a bad sore throat and it pained to swallow. The doctor recommended taking 50 mg of Demerol before meals. Two doctors looked in on me each day, Dr. Phil McGlave and Dr. Jeff Rank. They had looked at a blood smear on the slide: new cells were being made!! A great sign!! Bone marrow was being made in the spleen and liver and on its way to the proper sites. They said that this was one of the earliest "takes" they had seen. Glory to God and Only Him!!

October 17 "Day 12". . . I did about 30 push-ups in

the morning. My sore throat seemed to be getting constantly worse. I was feeling pretty good except for a cold sore that appeared on my lip plus a couple on my chin. Also I got sores on the roof of my mouth. What next? Herpes! This was nothing out of the ordinary — it occurs quite often.

October 18—"Day 13" . . . My mouth sores and sore throat sure were a hardship, every swallow pained me. I'd take the Demerol before meals, force down the food and then fall asleep. My white blood count now is 800. This gave me hope that maybe everything was going to turn out okay but it sure seemed like a rough road still ahead.

October 19—"Day 14" . . . I started on a new Herpes medication called Acyclovir for the sores on my lips, chin and in my mouth — ointment for the external ones and IV medication through the Hickman catheter. I made a couple more mats and another belt. Mary and Ellie were always encouraging me to do things, although I wasn't too thrilled about it. The reception on the television was very poor and the air filter was noisy so that it was hard to listen to tapes or the radio. We watched no TV and listened to very little radio. Time dragged on very slowly! Inside I felt jealous of the people that are healthy. The ones laughing, working and walking about. I wondered when I'd be doing the same.

October 20—"Day 15" . . . About the same as the previous day.

October 21—"Day 16" . . . Days are going by. We are both so lonesome for home and we miss the girls a lot! Sometimes we wonder if we should have had them visit us more often. It's hard to know what is best. It would be hard for them to see me in this condition — head shaved, no beard, thin. They had never come to visit me in the hospital through my other ordeal. It has been easier for Mary being here everyday. I was switched to a different pain medication. Dilaudid. It seemed to work a bit better than Demerol.

October 22—"Day 17"...Thank you, Jesus!!! All glory to Thee, dear Heavenly Father!! White blood count is 1,300!!! Another Praise the Lord!! The girls came to see us today. Jim and Bette brought them. Mary went down to the lobby to meet them. We were so glad to see each other — hugs and tears!!! I tried to be jolly for them but I knew my appearance would be a shock no matter how we had prepared them for it. They were sad to see Dad like this but knew they would keep praying so I could come home soon. It was hard for us all to say good-bye.

October 23—"Day 18"...White blood count 2,200!! The doctors were very pleased with my progress. It still seems a hard and long road for me but I have been uplifted in my spirit knowing that many are holding me up to the Heavenly Father in prayer. *Cards* and *more cards* have poured in. Mary has used them to decorate the walls of my room and I can't help but be cheered to know how much I'm remembered. Ellie also brought posters and sewed new curtains for the door. She has been such an inspiration to Mary and me. She has been here *every day* to encourage us on and bolster our spirits. She is a gem!! She would remind us to take one day at a time and to know that the Lord was with us and many, many were praying.

October 24—"Day 19"...Guess what? I ate all 3 meals today without pain medication! Things seem to be going better. The herpes, which I've had for a week now, are beginning to dry up.

October 25—"Day 20"... As of today, I have lost 16 pounds and the mouth sores are still troublesome. It has been a very sad day for Mary and me. Our friend from the next room, Connie Jambor, passed away due to complications. She, too, had a bone marrow transplant. Mary visited her and got to know her husband, John, as families of the patients shared their trials in the hallways. Our hearts just ache for him and his family. He had been in to encourage me many times. This has been a very depressing day for us and frightening with the thought of complications always overshadowing us. May God comfort and strengthen the Jambor family!

October 26—"Day 21"...Still depressed from yesterday.

October 27—"Day 22"...Depression lingers on. The doctors reduced my Prednisone. Hoping for discharge.

October 28—"Day 23"...THURSDAY — Thank you, Jesus!! Praise the Lord!! Discharge Day!! I had a bone marrow test done by Dr. Rank at 9:00 a.m. I almost crushed Mary's hand as I held it because of the pain during the procedure. A "discharge meeting" was held at 12:00 noon where they warned us and instructed us concerning things we might experience. We had to stay a week in Minneapolis so we were very thankful to be able to move in with Edward and Ellie. Their daughter, Laurie, gave up her room for us. It felt so good to be "home" with relatives and it seemed a miracle that Mary and I could be out for a short walk breathing fresh air! I had to go back to the clinic on Monday for a check up. Ellie was our constant, ready and willing chauffeur. How would we ever have gotten along without her! How blessed we were to have Ellie there. May God reward her!

Thursday was another clinic day. It was also another day of praise — we got to go home — home to Esko — home to our girls. We were referred to Dr. Robert Niedringhaus at the Duluth Clinic for our follow-up visits. Upon arriving home, the girls had "Welcome Home" banners all over the house. One goal I had was to be able to show up at the first day of basketball practice on November 8th. I slipped into the gym and sat in a corner and watched for a while. I didn't talk to anyone...it just seemed like a miracle being there.

MARY'S EXPERIENCE AND LEARNING AT JOHN'S BEDSIDE
By: "Gram"

Proverbs 31:28 "Her children arise and call her blessed; her husband also, and he praises her."

Being Mary's mother, I have marvelled how wonderfully God has sustained her through these years. She has been a true helpmeet to John and has been *continually* at his bedside through every hospital stay. He praises her courage and loving care — without which he says he may not have "made it". To see your loved one suffering — not knowing what the outcome will be — but still with patience and love encouraging him on and giving him hope! Only by supernatural strength can one continue and it is then you realize the power of prayer in your behalf.

For families staying with patients in a hospital setting, day in and day out, it is like living in a "world apart". You meet and become friends with those going through similar trials. You cry and rejoice together. Some die — others are discharged with great hope for the life ahead.

Mary had a course in nursing that she hadn't planned. She has learned "first hand" countless medical terms and the need for certain medications as she kept her "daily journal". She personally witnessed the trauma and loss of hospital friends — but also the joy of progress. Life itself puts on a different meaning and you learn to appreciate each precious moment.

Chapter V

Graft vs. Host Disease

Even during my days of depression and discouragement, I looked to the Word of God for strength and comfort. I knew there were *many faithful friends* continually praying for me. I loved my wife and family and I had a will to live, but if it was God's will to take me, I was ready!

> "I eagerly expect and hope that I will in no way be ashamed, but will have sufficient courage so that now as always Christ will be exalted in my body, whether by life or by death. For me to live is Christ and to die is gain."
>
> Philippians 1:20,21

Phil Johnson, a friend and neighbor, visited me faithfully many times a week sharing Scripture, praying and encouraging me on. There were many sleepless nights when I could relate to these words —"On my bed I remember you; I think of you through the watches of the night. Because you are my help, I sing in the shadow of your wings." Psalms 63:6,7.

All along I had a feeling within that the road ahead wasn't going to be a smooth one. Sure enough, eighteen days later I was back in Minneapolis at the clinic. I was having headaches all the time and my white count and hemoglobin were both low. That's why I was tired all the time and I was also having a bad sore throat. Next, my white count went high — I was fighting some infection. So what happens next? The sore throat was diagnosed as herpes and I have to come to the clinic every 8 hours for Acyclovir again for 7 days. We stayed at Ed and Ellie's for two days in Minneapolis, then came home and continued the treatment in Duluth.

It seemed a bother to be going to Duluth every 8 hours — fifteen miles away — but it was better than being hospitalized. My throat was getting better and so were the blood counts.

"Day 51" was Thanksgiving Day, November 25th. I had so much to be thankful for. Thank you, God! Thank you, Jesus! Thank you for life! Thank you, Tom!

Five days after Thanksgiving I was back at the University of Minnesota Clinic to see Dr. McGlave. He was checking for Graft versus Host disease. This occurs when my new bone marrow (the graft) recognizes my body (the host) as foreign and tries to attack it. Three target areas are the skin, intestinal tract and the liver. It can occur up to several months after the transplant. He did a skin biopsy and verified Graft versus Host rash on my upper trunk and arms. He prescribed some special cream. We stayed overnight again at Ed and Ellie's and went to the clinic again the next day. We were then allowed to go home.

In the beginning of December, the rash began to spread to my legs, feet and forearms and my ankles were also swollen. Along with this I had a bad sore throat and a deep cough. Having this rash was very frightening. I had come to know a forty year old man who had been discharged from the bone marrow unit but who later died of severe Graft vs. Host and complications. This fear seemed to hang over me like a cloud but I still trusted in God to deliver me. Again it happened — what I dreaded most!! I was admitted back into the University of Minnesota Hospital on December

12th—68 days after the transplant. My throat and mouth looked bad... seemed like herpes for the third time. I was barely eating. The rash was somewhat under control but my skin was very dry and peeling. I was put on Acyclovir again. Mary was faithfully by my side and Gram was staying with our girls and holding "down the fort".

My liver function count was higher than normal so a liver biopsy was done on the 15th of December. It showed mild Graft vs. Host disease in the liver. I was started back on Prednisone along with Penicillin. My throat gradually improved and although my cough still lingered, I was discharged from the hospital on December 19th after a week's stay. I still had to travel back and forth to Duluth for my Acyclovir until the 26th. I felt really bad about not being able to attend my brother-in-law, Phil and Julie's wedding on December 4, 1982. Mary and the girls took part in it and were filled with excitement but they tended to be more subdued around me.

Although I was glad to be at home, it was hard to get into the excitement and spirit of Christmas. This all just added turmoil and unrest in the family. (Living with illness touches every member of the family and calls for much sacrifice and patience.) The girls had to adjust to quiet, low-key day to day living with the underlying tension. I'm sure they didn't fully enjoy the holidays. As a secret goal to bring in the New Year, I had wanted to go snowmobiling with John Bonneville. I was glad to be able to do that! John and Marie went with Mary and me. It was just great to be in the outdoors and seemed a dream that I was actually able to do it!

In January of 1983, I went for my 100 day check-up. Doctors feel if you reach this goal things look very hopeful. My usual weight is about 168-170 pounds but I was maintaining only around 153 pounds. I still had

Graft vs. Host disease in my mouth and my face was still puffy and reddish in color. My hair was coming in quite well. The bone marrow test checked out okay and the Hickman Catheter was removed. It is a fantastic medical invention but I was ever so grateful to have it removed.

I was able to come back to do some coaching starting in February. Mr. Bob Swanstrom and Mr. John Bonneville had been taking over for me. Going back to the coaching duties was very traumatic! Here I was walking into the gym with my "stocking cap" on and weighing about 25 pounds less than normal. The cap stayed on for a few days and then I changed to a "fatigue cap". Boy oh boy, did I look like a guerilla "hit-man" then with my dark sunglasses! (I had to wear them because of sensitive eyes.) Other coaches and friends said I looked very, very mean. Finally the day came when I felt I had to go to basketball practice without a hat. I got the courage to flip it up on the bleachers! Immediately I could see the girls looking and talking so I called my Assistant Coach Bonneville over. I told him to go and tell the girls to make a joke about my head and the pressure and tension would be over. A few minutes later they all yelled in unison, "Welcome back, Cueball!" Boy, I thought to myself, I didn't have much discipline that time! That was all it took—they welcomed me back with open arms.

A Benefit Basketball Night was held for me on February 12, 1983, in the school gymnasium. In great numbers the people of the community and surrounding areas came to show their love and give me moral support. I was deeply touched by this occasion and their caring!

This event which was organized by Bob Swanstrom, required a lot of hard work. He did an excellent job in preparing the games, contacting participants, printing of the bulletins and advertising and in arranging the night's program. He and John Bonneville have meant a lot to me! I hope that they and everyone know my "thanks" goes deeper than mere words.

I didn't look or feel the best and even hesitated about attending. But — the love which we as a family felt from everyone, will always have a special place of remembrance in our hearts! God bless you all — your love and friendship will be rewarded.

JOHN GRUSSENDORF BENEFIT BASKETBALL NIGHT

When: Saturday evening, February 12 beginning at 7:00

Where: The new gymnasium at Esko High School.

Donation: $2.00 donation at the door plus optional 50¢ chances for the half-time youth and adult "Hot Shot" spot shooting contests.

Why: This is a benefit to help John Grussendorf, Esko's head girls' basketball coach, defray mounting medical expenses resulting from 2 major operations. Within the past year, John has undergone massive intestinal surgery as well as a delicate bone marrow transplant. People who feel moved to assist John and his family during this critical time are asked to attend this benefit. For people unable to attend, but moved to contribute, individual donations could be mailed directly to John Grussendorf, 190 N. Cloquet Road, Esko, Minnesota 55733.

What: An unusual basketball game will be played in a *lighter atmosphere* where area girls' basketball coaches, and girl athletes themselves turn out to help one of their own. The first half action will pit the Lake Superior Conference plus Superior A and B squad girls' basketball coaches directed by Dick Swanson against the Polar League along with Wrenshall and Albrook head and assistant girls' coaches mentored by Maury Veilleux. Here's a rare opportunity for the girl basketball players in the Duluth-Superior and surrounding areas to come to Esko to watch their coaches strut their stuff.

Half-time will feature "Hot Shot" sport shooting contests in both youth and adult categories for the $25.00 grand prize.

The second half will highlight the girl athletes from our area as the College of St. Scholastica womens' basketball team coached by Kris Sheldon-Purcell will take on the Esko girls' basketball alumni team directed by Ellie Randels, Esko's former girls' head basketball coach. This is a chance to see many of our area's fine girl athletes who are now playing small college basketball at Scholastica play the Lady Eskomos of yesterday.

Mark Stodghill, sports reporter for the *Duluth*

Herald & News-Tribune, will handle the public address play by play with color commentary being provided by a mystery local celebrity. Bob Peterson of Esko and Andy Coathup from Cloquet will officiate. Rod Johnson will be the official scorer and timer. The present Esko girls' basketball A and B team members will be working in all areas of the benefit as well.

This promises to be a light, memorable night dedicated to Coach John Grussendorf, and girls' basketball up here in the Northland.

POLAR LEAGUE COACHES TEAM

Danny Nelson—Wrenshall
Dave Stoltenburg—Wrenshall
Randy Myhre—Barnum
Larry Anderson—Albrook
Debbie Doble—Albrook
Bob Emerson—Carlton
Randy Thudin—Carlton
Dan Bottaglia—Askov
Steve Schoenbauer—Askov
Becky Dooley—Floodwood
Oscar Eliason—Cromwell
John Bonneville—Esko
Kerry Juntunen—Esko
Bob Swanstrom—Esko

VS
LAKE SUPERIOR COACHES TEAM

Bob Lahti—Duluth Central
Maggie Dittburner—Duluth Central
Ken Schloer—Cloquet
Dave Bergett—Cloquet
Jim Zack—Cloquet
Keith Levinski—Cloquet
Mary Freeman—Proctor
Warren Peterson—Denfeld-Morgan Park
Mike Scrignoli—Denfeld-Morgan Park
Tom Bang—Hermantown
Dawn Tafe—Hermantown
Keith Swanson—Hermantown
Buzz Delarosby—Two Harbors
Richie Peterson—Proctor

St. SCHOLASTICA SAINTS

11 Mary Koglin—Hermantown, Minnesota
13 Cookie Crim—Green Bay, Wisconsin
21 Peggy Hess—Staples, Minnesota
23 Robin Anderson—Carlton, Minnesota
31 Brenda Johnson—Duluth, Minnesota
33 Lisa Ziegler—Hermantown, Minnesota
35 Hannah Tjader—Ely, Minnesota
41 Sarah Sinniger—LaCrosse, Wisconsin
43 Terry Lauer—Staples, Minnesota
45 Brenda Rogalski—Crystal Falls, MI
53 Kim Juntunen—Esko, Minnesota
55 Eva Polkoski—Iron River, Wisconsin
15 Colleen Gilchrist—Cloquet, Minnesota
   Mary Kay Hohensee—Carlton, Minnesota
   Coaches: Kris Sheldon-Purcell
            El Randels

VS

ALUMNI ROSTER

Jeanne Sunnarborg 1969—Brooklyn Center
Mary Murto Lee 1970—Esko
Karen Antonson Carlton 1971—Esko
Terry Koski Colalillo 1971—Duluth
Diane Lahti Ritchie 1972—Cloquet
Jill Kinghorn Bang 1972—Cloquet
Linda Warren 1974—Esko
Becky Koski VanHout 1974—Cloquet
Eileen Hanson Heikkila 1974—Floodwood
Renee Flynn Swanson 1974—Barnum
Robin Flynn Theisen 1975—Barnum
Sue Heaslip Chinn 1976—Cloquet
Lynn Meyer 1976—Duluth
Judy VanWave 1977—Esko
Carol Erickson Szyman 1977—Cloquet
Kelli Tatro 1977—Esko
Mary Meyer 1978—Esko
Sandy Burggraff 1978—Esko
Diane Wutz 1978—Duluth

Wendy Stonemark Lyytinen 1978—Cloquet Manager
Karen Meyer 1979—Maplewood
Sue East 1979—Roseville
Joy Pykkonen 1979—Esko
Jane Koivisto 1979—Duluth
Sharyl Geisert 1979—Moorhead
Karla Meyer 1980—Duluth
Lori Lindstrom Hudspith 1980—Bovey
Brenda Flynn 1980—Esko
Mary Meger 1980—Duluth
Sandy Puumala 1981—Esko
Sam Munter 1981—Ely
Sara Solwold Johnson 1981—Cloquet
Sally Granholm 1982—Esko

BASKETBALL TRIVIA

Eli Umpierre shot during a game while sitting on the floor?
We first saw the new coaches?
Remember summer practices and shooting 200 shots a day?
The whole team went to practice in our pajamas during Christmas vacation?
Some of the players thought it would be fun to wear band-aids with smiles on them on their legs?
The rule about wearing a stocking hat?
The team members had to be in their houses by 9:30 the night before the game?
We all gave the coaches a kiss on Valentine's Day! (A Hershey's kiss that is)
We had to run 30 sprints after a game because the other team scored 10 points above our defensive goal? (even though we won)
Mr. Grussendorf's saying "The more I yell at you the more I love you!" and "If I don't yell I wouldn't care."

The whole team wants to thank our coaches for making our basketball careers a time for learning and fun. We love our coaches!!

Duluth News-Tribune & Herald, Sunday, February 13, 1983

ESKO COACH TOUGH; HE FOUGHT DEATH

by Mark Stodghill

"I don't consider it a successful first day of practice unless a half-dozen girls have to run to the bathroom."

—John Grussendorf, Esko Girls Basketball Coach

BEFORE YOU start an angry letter to the editor saying "who does this guy think he is, pushing girls so hard that they get sick?" Listen to Eli Umpierre, starting guard on Esko's 15-1 Polar League-leading girls basketball team.

"He runs us hard, but in the fourth quarter of a game it pays off," she said. "We love it. Our parents love it. They see how tired we are when we get home and they know that when we play a game we're going to be in shape to play. When I go home I'm so tired I just eat, go into my room, turn on the electric blanket and rest. He's tough on us, but we like it."

Grussendorf has a lot of people who either like or respect him. That's why Esko assistant girls basketball coaches Bob Swanstrom and John Bonneville and the Lake Superior Conference and Polar League girls basketball coaches held a benefit basketball game for him at Esko Saturday night. Before we get to why the man was so honored, here's more on the coach.

Grussendorf coached boys basketball for 14 years before switching to the Esko girls three seasons ago. He had only one goal with the girls. "I saw the capabilities of the girls," he said. "My first year I said, 'If you don't want to play like boys, don't come out.' I wanted them to play as close to a boys team as they could."

And if he had to put them through more physical tests than a drill sergeant to achieve that goal, so be it. Grussendorf would make the girls the best that they could be.

The 37-year-old Hermantown native is an "old school" coach. He's a throwback to the days when players had to relate to the coaches and not vice versa.

"My job is to separate the scrub oak from the evergreen," Grussendorf said in explaining his coaching philosophy. "I admit my program isn't for every girl, but I believe in it. If you treat kids fair, they love discipline. If I would go into another school without the athletic tradition of Esko, I would never get away with this. But these people know what it takes to be winners."

HERE ARE some of the things Grussendorf thinks it takes to be a winner:

• Bed checks the night before a game. If a girl is not home and doesn't return the phone call of one of Grussendorf's managers by 10 p.m., she'll do a sprint for every minute she's late. He once made a girl do 40 sprints.

• If one of the Eskomo girls is caught outside without a hat, there might be more running or even a week-long suspension from the team. "It's a health thing to keep them from getting colds and it also shows that the girls are a team," Grussendorf says.

• When in doubt, run. "I'm an advocate of conditioning," Grussendorf says. "I go overboard." If a team out-conditions his girls, it's his fault. So he won't let it happen.

But the Esko girls have learned that they can push, condition and discipline themselves to put up with just about anything Grussendorf dishes out. The coach says he hopes that carries over to the rest of their lives.

There's no better example than the one their teacher has set.

IN THE past 11 months, Grussendorf has pushed himself back from the death bed once and has won a gamble to stay away from it a second time.

Last March, he underwent major surgery called Parks-Pouch procedure, for ulcerative colitis. His large intestine was removed and the last three loops of the small intestine were rebuilt into a pouch, but there were complications.

"They couldn't find where the bleeding started and my body cavity filled with blood. They didn't know how to stop it," he said. "I went through 49 units of blood and had respiratory arrest. But there was a miracle from the Lord. The bleeding stopped and even the doctors don't know how."

Grussendorf won that battle. Another one loomed for the father of four daughters ages 13, 12, 11 and 9.

Seven months after his stomach surgery, Grussendorf took a blood test and it was discovered that he had aplastic anemia, a disease in which the bone marrow shuts down and quits producing.

He underwent a bone marrow transplant last October. Radiation was used to kill the old bone marrow and he received a bone marrow transplant from his younger brother, Tom. The transplant was a success. One of the wonders of the procedure is that John now has Tom's A-positive blood type instead of his old O-negative.

But as a result of the transplant John developed Graft vs. Host disease in which his body fought the new bone marrow.

IT HASN'T been a fun past 4½ months. First he lost his hair because of the radiation treatments. His skin darkened like a man who was tanned and had spent too much time in the sun. His fingernails started to fall out. Then his immunities were down and something as simple as a cold or flu could be critical.

Two of the four people on his floor at the hospital died after having the same delicate surgery.

"I remember when the one guy left the hospital," Grussendorf related. "He was 47 years old and when he checked out he came by my room, pumped his fists in the air and said, 'Hang in there John. I've got the world by the tail.' Then he died. Even with a Christian background and faith, I wanted to quit. The bottom just about fell out.

". . . I don't know why I had to go through this but the answer will be shown to me some day. I'm a born-again Christian and that faith, the prayers of people and my wife (Mary) — especially her, she was more than a peach, she was a real trooper — got me through this."

It looks as though John has gotten through it. He expects to be back in top shape by April 1 to help his three brothers, who are partners in a Hermantown landscaping business, gear up for the busy season.

The medical bills have mounted, though. He figures somewhere around $100,000. He has insurance but "a few thousand" will be coming out of his pocket. That's why his friends and fellow coaches held the benefit game Saturday night.

Grussendorf recently returned to basketball practice and isn't afraid to say that the girls had developed nicely without him. He credits Swanstrom and Bonneville for that. "Bob and John did just a super job going 12-1. I'll probably lose five in a row now," he said on his return.

The Eskomos have won three in a row since Grussendorf's return and have clinched at least a tie for the Polar League championship.

His coming out or back wasn't without it's uneasy moments. At first, Grussendorf wore a stocking cap to hide his hairless head. Then he switched to a fatigue cap. Finally he discarded that.

"I looked over in the corner and some of the girls were kind of whispering and pointing," Grussendorf said. "I told John Bonneville to go over there and have them make up a joke." They all hollered, "Welcome back, cueball!"

"If you would have saw that, you wouldn't have thought much of my discipline. But they got their laugh and that was the end of it."

Umpierre says things ran smoothly under Swanstrom and Bonneville, but the girls are glad to have Grussendorf back. "Mr. Swanstrom is a really good coach, but he's kind of mellow," Umpierre explained. "Mr. Bonneville is kind of between Mr. Grussendorf and Mr. Swanstrom.

Mr. Grussendorf hollers a lot and expects a lot. When he first came back (teammate) Deb Mattinen said, 'Hey, he's sure yelling a lot!' I said, 'Yeah, I love it.' She said, 'I do too.' "

The yelling won't stop and neither will the running as long as Grussendorf is calling the shots.

When practice starts next season he'll again push the girls to their stomach's limits.

"You'd think they'd wise up and eat a big meal before practice. Then it wouldn't take as long," he said. There was a trace of a smile.

We went on to win our last five games of the regular season plus three tournament games. We were District Champions, finally losing to Biwabik in the region opener. The season ended with twenty victories and two losses. I had to consider that season a tremendous success, not only in the win column but in witnessing, sharing and caring by my athletes, fellow coaches and friends. The Lord sure works in mysterious ways His wonders to perform. I am so thankful that I have Jesus Christ in my heart as my own personal Saviour! Praise the Lord for that!

It had been a long grind and still 5½ months after the transplant things were touch and go. I was having a cough, runny nose and feeling tired. My temperature rose to 102 so we decided to see Dr. Niedringhaus in Duluth. After he adjusted the intake of several drugs which I had been on, my blood count went back into the normal range and things began to get better. Six months after the transplant all of my counts were normal — white count 9,400, hemoglobin 11.9 and platelets 273,000. We thank God for the wisdom and knowledge of the medical profession and we praise God for His healing hand!

Seven months after transplant — end of the basketball season and end of the school year — May 1983, the Athletic Banquet and Awards Night was a big event at the Esko School. I handed out awards and gave a short testimony and thanked everyone for their love and concern and also for their prayers in my behalf.

During the summer of 1983 I was back to work at the nursery. My immune system wasn't completely back to normal so I had to use caution in being exposed to the sun. It was awkward for me to wear long sleeve shirts and to wear a cap at all times. I had to rest in the shade and to use sun screen! It was very difficult at times because of my love for the good old sunshine!!

In September of 1983, not quite one year after the transplant, Mary and I went to do a planting job in Hamilton, Montana, with Phil and Julie. It was to do some landscaping at the Riverbend Racquetball Club. We spent five enjoyable days there working and renewing friendships.

From November 1983 to March 1984 I coached the Esko Girls Varsity Basketball Team. John Bonneville was my assistant again and Brent Smith coached the 9th grade girls with Kathy Munter in the 7th and 8th grade level. It was an exciting year especially with all four of my daughters playing and involved in the basketball program. Miranda as an eighth grader, Angela in seventh and Brenda and Tanya involved in the elementary.

Chapter VI

Third Overtime

In April of 1984 I was feeling very good and was back working with the crew at the nursery besides doing estimates. The summer went well. The bone marrow was working fine and the pouch was working adequately with help from a little medication.

November began and John Bonneville continued as my assistant. We looked forward to another basketball season. This fifth year of coaching girls started out fine. Three of the starters had graduated and one had moved away. Things went smoothly until the second game of the district tournaments. Then bingo — another death threat!!!

We were into the District Tournaments at Proctor High School. It was Saturday, February 23, 1985. We had played Albrook in the afternoon and won which put us into the semi-finals. I went back in the evening to watch the two games and also to help out at the tournament by keeping an eye on the locker rooms.

On Sunday morning we attended church as a family. In the afternoon Mary went to lie down to rest as she had a sore throat. When she awoke about 3 o'clock, she found me on the couch with five blankets piled on top of me by the girls. I had such bad chills and my temperature was 103. Finally the chills left me and I just felt a little sick. We came to the conclusion that it must be the 'flu bug'. Flu — you bet!!

Monday morning the girls went off to school. I called Mr. Bonneville in the morning to tell him I had a bad sore throat and that he would probably have to handle basketball practice on his own. I wasn't feeling much better so I did take a penicillin pill seeing that I had one left from a recent treatment for sore throat. Mary called Dr. Niedringhaus' office about 9 a.m. hoping to get a prescription. We hadn't received a reply by 12 o'clock so she called again. They were just about to call us to say that the doctor wanted to see me — appointment time was set for 4 o'clock.

Mary had been busy all morning in the basement with the usual Monday wash. I had stayed in bed until noon when I went to sit in the recliner in the living room. Mary tried to take my temperature but it wouldn't even come close to being normal. She just assumed that the thermometer wasn't working right. Then she took one look at me and said we'd better go in immediately — we can't wait until 4 p.m. My nose, ears, fingers and toes were starting to turn blue. Mary said afterwards that she had been puzzled by this and remembered our daughter Angela's fingernails beginning to discolor when she had the croup and wasn't getting enough oxygen. Little did we know what lay ahead of us!

I didn't feel up to driving, which is unusual, so Mary drove to the Duluth Clinic. I insisted on being dropped off while she went to park. I stopped on the first floor to buy an inhaler as my nose felt stuffy and I was having a difficult time breathing. I couldn't open it because my fingers were numb so I just shoved it into my pocket.

By the time Mary came I was on the third floor having routine blood work done. They were having a very difficult time drawing blood because of the lack of oxygen—my veins kept collapsing. She saw a wheelchair being brought in and the next thing she knew I was wheeled out in the chair. Mary related later that she was bewildered and shocked to see my coloring getting worse and I didn't look good at all. She wheeled me to the second floor to get a chest x-ray. This was all routine orders. After waiting our turn, we finally were back on the third floor to see Dr. Niedringhaus. I got up out of the wheelchair and brought my x-rays to the desk to be checked. I went back to sit in a regular chair, waiting for the doctor.

Mary could see how sick I was with dark blotches beginning to appear on my forehead. She went in and insisted to the nurse that I was very, very sick and must see the doctor right away. I was brought back into a room and she went and got Dr. Niedringhaus from another patient. He took one look at me — he knew I was *seriously ill.* He asked some brief questions and then informed us that I'd have to be *admitted immediately* to the Intensive Care Unit at St. Mary's Hospital. He didn't smooth things over. He frankly said it was very serious and could be life-threatening. We must act quickly!! (Dr. Niedringhaus later told me that I had taken 10 years off his life the way I looked when he walked into the room. He said that I was the sickest anybody has ever been who has walked into the clinic on his own two feet.)

Mary and I were in shock! How could this be — our world was falling apart!! We just couldn't believe what we were hearing — life threatening — have to get oxygen and antibiotics *immediately!!* Judging by my appearance, we were told it could be a quick acting pneumonia. Mary went to the doctor while he was making the hospital arrangements and asked if she should notify our daughters and family relatives. He answered, "not at this point". She came back to me and we wept in each others arms, completely bewildered!

The nurse wheeled me rapidly across the skywalk to the hospital. Mary had a hard time keeping up and later realized the urgency of it all. The nurse was very careful in her choice of words and just apologized and said that she always walks fast. What made things more traumatic was that a friend of ours had just recently passed away at the age of 42. As we arrived at the ICU, it was the exact place where I had just been days before and visited him. You can imagine what thoughts were racing through our minds!!

When we arrived at the ICU the bed for me was all prepared. As the nurses began to get me ready for treatment, Mary went to the lounge to make a call to her Mom. Gram knew we had gone for a supposed checkup but was horrified to hear that my condition now was life threatening. Mary asked her to have Phil get our girls from basketball practice and to come to the hospital immediately. Before Phil came to pick her up, Gram had made a few quick phone calls to family, neighbor Jane and Pastor Hilman telling them of my condition and requesting they start a prayer chain. How comforting and blessed to be able to call on faithful prayer warriors! Mary also called Tom's wife, Sandie, and asked her to notify my Dad and Mom and the rest of the family.

Mary came back to my room and we talked briefly. The nurses were still busy setting up the IV and oxygen, etc. Dr. Niedringhaus had called in other specialists to confer with. We overheard such phrases as kidney shutdown, blood poisoning, etc. which brought us frightening memories of the trying days of our friend, Jack.

Phil and Gram had arrived with the girls. They came into the room to see their Dad. They were shocked at all the tubes and bewildered to see Dad in such a condition. How could this thing have happened so quickly? Dad was at home when they had left for school in the morning.

Soon the waiting room was filled with people bewildered and shocked by the news — Mom and Dad Grussendorf, the brothers and their wives, Pastor Hilman, Mary's brothers and their wives, and the coaches John Bonneville and Rod Johnson along with their wives. I'm sure they were all praying in my behalf.

It was a very crucial time! The doctors found out that I had septicemia (blood poisoning) and not pneumonia as they had earlier thought. The poisoning had gone throughout my whole system. Due to that one last penicillin pill I had taken, the doctors weren't able to diagnose the cause and therefore treated me with various antibiotics so that I was completely covered. I was told later that taking it was a large factor in helping me to survive. My condition at this time was very critical. My blood pressure was being regulated by medication and my temperature was low and my kidneys were on the verge of shut down! I was dying!!!

(as told by Mary)

The girls seemed so lost and bewildered — wandering around not knowing what to do! Miranda, our oldest daughter, called me aside and asked, "Is Dad going to die? Tell me the truth. Don't lie." Words can't describe my feelings as I answered, "I don't know." How my heart ached for her and the other girls — but there was sweet comfort to them and to me to have others near to help us pass away these agonizing moments! No words needed to be said. We knew that everyone was in constant prayer for John. John's brothers went into the ICU periodically to give him encouragement. Pastor Hilman had been in John's room to pray over him. Gram, Phil and I had gone into the prayer room where we wept and prayed for John's healing and for wisdom for the doctors. Through many trials we had experienced the comfort of being able to kneel before the Almighty and pour out our hearts to Him! Then we received an uplifting telephone call! John's brother, Carl, took the message. We were informed that John's basketball players, some of their parents, and also some of our church board members were gathered at the church in Esko praying for John! Praise God! Others had joined us and Heaven was being "stormed" with prayers and supplications!!

All this while, the doctors had been busy working with John and consulting on procedures. Praise God for their wisdom and knowledge in caring for the sick! After several hours, which to us seemed an eternity, Dr. Niedringhaus gave us the report that we could all breathe a little easier. John's blood pressure, kidney function, etc. had leveled off — although he still wasn't 'out of the woods'. Praise God — there's power in prayer!! The Lord stopped John's system from deteriorating! He had heard our prayers! A while later the doctor told us we could go home. We all held hands as Pastor Hilman led us in a prayer of praise and thanksgiving to God. We all trusted that things had turned for the better.

I knew I couldn't leave — I had to stay with John. Marie Bonneville offered to stay with me but I thanked her and said I'd be okay. To our surprise, John had remembered to ask them to drive our car home. It was still parked in front of the clinic. They were happy to do this favor for us.

The girls, Phil and Gram took turns in going to see John before they left. Others left also. It was good to know that Gram was in charge of the girls again at home. Words can't express my gratitude to all those who helped the girls and me, by their presence and prayers, through those first trying hours.

The night seemed so long! Here I was again, back at my post, trying to encourage John to battle against yet another disease. I know in my own strength I couldn't do it, but again I was being upheld by many prayers and God has renewed my strength and given me courage to brave this trial and be of help to John. The time passed as I'd go back and forth to check on him and then rest awhile in the lounge. The discoloring seemed to be disappearing from his forehead, mouth and ears. His fingers, nose and toes still remained blue. He complained of a bad sore throat and stuffy nose.

Morning came and he seemed pretty good. Then all of a sudden he broke into a cold, clammy sweat. His blood pressure went way up and suddenly dropped. The nurses were having trouble regulating it and talked of calling the doctor. This caused me to become alarmed and I called Gram to come with the girls as soon as she could. I called Sandie also. This may have been a wrong decision on my part but it was my reaction because of what we had just experienced. By the time Gram and Phil arrived with the girls, the nurses had found the problem and John's blood pressure was stabilized. We visited in the lounge and the girls took turns going in to see Dad. Miranda, the oldest, preferred just staying in the lounge area, but she wanted to know exactly how everything was. I know she realized the seriousness of it all. John's feet looked really bad. They were swollen to above the ankles and purple in color. His fingers were also a purple color but the coloring of his nose seemed better. We hoped things would gradually improve. It was reassuring to see the doctors and nurses — I know they were doing their utmost! It was also comforting to have family around to help share the burden. All the while, we knew that word was spreading concerning John's illness and there would be hundreds more praying! How uplifting the thought of it!!

Miranda wanted to stay close by and suggested that she'd stay with me at the hospital over night. The other girls then left with Gram and Phil. I really enjoyed having her there. She wanted to do her part by just being there. She got our cots ready and we talked awhile before going to sleep. I got up several times during the night to check on John.

John already had a sore throat before being hospitalized. It seemed to be getting better with all the antibiotics and his appetite had improved. Then, all of a sudden, the throat got worse again and Dr. Niedringhaus seemed a bit puzzled. He called in Dr. Portilla, an ear, nose and throat specialist. After further investigation, they discovered little sores farther down in the back of the throat. Sinus x-rays showed a bad infection. The doctors felt that John's septicemia may have come from either strep-throat or sinus infection or a combination.

At this time John didn't have the strength to undergo more extensive work so Dr. Portilla did some minor surgery to remove the crusting from the nostrils and also to clean and flush out the sinuses.

During the first days in the ICU, John walked around quite well although his feet hurt. With each day the pain became more and more severe and no amount of painkiller would bring relief. It took him a good half hour to get up from a lying position and stand beside the bed so he could use the commode. Thoughts of amputation crossed all of our minds, doctors included. I tried to cover up my feelings and fears with positive thoughts as I constantly kept reassuring John that his feet would be back to normal.

During all these days the girls had managed to get rides to the hospital so they could visit their Dad. One evening Mom and Dad Grussendorf came to spend the evening at the hospital while I went with our girls to attend the Girls Basketball Tournament at Proctor. Miranda and Angela decided they would be up to playing. We let them decide for themselves. John felt that if his team saw me there, they would know the "Coach" was doing alright. My mind and heart really weren't on the game. I kept wondering how he was doing and it was really a relief when I got back to the hospital and found him sleeping!

The next evening, Saturday, we heard a bulletin by the weather service that a severe winter storm was headed our way. Sure enough, Sunday came with heavy snow and high winds. We surely couldn't expect company at the hospital now. The storm increased and prevented hospital personnel from coming in to work so the nurses on duty had to work double shifts. Dr. Niedringhaus had walked through the storm to come in and reported that traffic was at a standstill. Snowmobiles were being used for emergency service. John was supposed to be moved from the ICU on Monday but due to the limited staff, he stayed until Tuesday.

Sunday afternoon I received a shocking call from Minneapolis. Ellie, John's sister, said her husband, Edward, was in the Intensive Care Unit with a brain hemorrhage. I was asked to notify the rest of John's family.

When I got back from the nurses station John inquired anxiously about the call. It was so hard to break the news to him! How unbelievable that his brother-in-law would be going through such a trial! We immediately prayed for the Lord to spare his life and to be a comfort to Ellie and the family. Relatives kept in contact and then informed us on Edward's condition. How hard it is for us to understand God's ways!

A heat tent was tried to bring relief to the pain in John's feet. Even amid the pain there was a ray of hope and sunshine! — feeling had to be coming back. Thank the Lord for *pain!* Many times during the night he would have to sit up in bed and try to grab his feet in such a way as to ease the pain. He described it as if they were being pounded with a sledge hammer and pulled with a vice grip! He said it was the worst pain he has ever experienced.

During all this hospital stay, Pastor Hilman had

visited John every day! What a comfort and blessing he was to both of us. After seven days in the ICU, Tuesday was moving day into a private room. We were so thankful for the wonderful care he had received there but it was a joy to leave. It was a hopeful sign of progress! We moved all the lovely plants, flowers and cards to the new room.

John still had a lot of pain in his feet. He would always remind everyone to be careful not to bump them, especially when he went around with the wheelchair across the skywalk to the clinic for x-rays. A visit by the kidney doctor left us reassured that everything was fine in that department.

After five days in the private room, things had improved so much that Saturday was to be "going home day"! Jim, John's brother, drove us. Tears of thankfulness flowed from my eyes as we neared our home. John had survived another critical and crucial episode. Praise the Lord!!!! Words can't explain the gratefulness in our hearts! We went home with a car full of flowers, plants and get well cards, tears of joy streaming down our faces. I thanked the Lord for allowing me to have John a little longer!

I wondered to myself how John would make it inside because of the pain in his feet. Ever so slowly he made it up the outside stairs. He was wearing a pair of cotton socks with a woolen pair over them (he couldn't wear shoes). It was indeed a good sign for him to have such pain. It meant that feeling and sensation were coming back. He walked on his heels because it was too painful to allow the toes to touch anything. He had been given a prescription of penicillin and antibiotics to be taken daily.

Gram and the girls were waiting for us with "WELCOME HOME" banners all over the house. We all cried and embraced each other, thanking God for yet another miracle! With a trembling voice John said,

"It's so good to be home!"

Gram had a meal prepared, the house cleaned, clothes washed etc. What would we have done without her? She was always so willing and ready to help and assist in any way possible — besides being such a comfort and companion to the girls!!! We pray God's blessings on her for all her love!

As the days went by John's health improved and he gained some of the weight he had lost through this ordeal. He did still have a hard time breathing and now that he was a bit stronger, Dr. Portilla decided it was time to try to relieve that condition. More sinus surgery was performed. The Doctor explained that larger sinus drainage openings or windows were made and part of the septum (cartilage between the nostrils) had to be removed which had deteriorated because of the septicemia. The previous surgery had been a minor cleanout. This one wasn't as easy — his face was swollen and he needed constant ice applications. Hopefully, all this would now solve the sinus problem!

After this we made frequent trips to the clinic for check-ups — John still using the wheelchair. Dr. Portilla cleaned out his nose and with each visit there was less to do. The dead tissue and crusted drainage was finally releasing itself and coming out gradually. By now, his nose condition and breathing were much improved and all the blood counts were excellent.

During these clinic check-ups, Dr. Niedringhaus always checked John's feet, etc. Finally the time came when he was able to *walk* into the clinic. Praise the Lord! I believe all the doctors were puzzled by his feet. They probably hadn't had a case like this before. While he was hospitalized, they had even taken pictures of them. If heat or hot water was applied, it would cause severe throbbing pain and cold applications would prevent the blood from circulating. John discovered that allowing them to be exposed to the air was the best.

I had asked Dr. Niedringhaus on one of our visits, if he was a little bit surprised how John's feet had improved. He replied, "Not a little bit surprised — a great deal surprised." He was amazed at the healing power in John's body.

Miranda was an unbelievably great help! She went the extra mile for her Dad. Every night she would put on lotion and massage his feet for an hour — always being very gentle and careful not to use too much pressure. I'm sure she was silently praying for healing as she did this.

John had lost all the nails on his toes and the old skin had died and turned black. Brand new soft pink skin formed on every toe along with new soft toe nails! The miracle of healing — truly of the Lord!! "I will praise Thee; for I am fearfully and wonderfully made." (Psalm 139:14) Now, three months later, he is feeling fine and working at the nursery. There's still one stubborn scab left on the tip of one toe but we know and believe that too will eventually have baby new skin and a new soft toe nail!!

After John came home from the hospital, he knew he had to share his "story" with others. First, to thank and praise the Lord and to give Him all the glory for His healing through the years — and secondly, to help console, comfort and encourage others who are struggling through hard times. He decided this was the best way to accomplish that, even though it would be quite an undertaking. He says: "There's something more important to me than athletics and being a successful Coach — and that is my relationship with Jesus Christ! Every coach has a dream to go to the State Tournament and participate in the great event. But more importantly — if one athlete whom I have been associated with comes to know the Lord as their own personal Saviour sometime down life's road — this to me means more than any State Tournament trip. The healing of the soul is more important than the healing of the body. *If only one person comes to know my Jesus, then all the pain and suffering I've had to bear is worth it."*

"I raised you up for this very purpose, that I might display my power in you and that my name might be proclaimed in all the earth."
Romans 9:17

Article from the Hermantown Star
(A Community Newspaper)
April 4, 1985

Be sure to read the article on John Grussendorf found in this week's *Hermantown Star.*

Grussendorf is a very, very special man, a guy who lives his life on faith. He is sincerely interested in young people.

"Drugs, alcohol, sex and peer pressure — it all is out there to rob the kids of their happiness," Grussendorf told me in an interview Saturday morning. "It's good that the kids see death up close through me. I hope that it helps them put their priorities in the right order."

I know that his testimony encouraged me. I hope his words brighten your day, too.

JOHN GRUSSENDORF HAS MORE TO TEACH THAN BASKETBALL SKILLS

By Guy Hanson

Job, n. in the Bible, a man who endured much suffering but did not lose his faith in God.
— Webster's Dictionary

You have to admire John Grussendorf's faith and courage.

Like Job, the biblical faith giant, Grussendorf has had his faith tested. Three illnesses over the past four years, each manifesting itself as a life-threatening condition, have helped build his faith in God.

Grussendorf, 39, is a deeply religious man. He does not hide the fact that he loves Jesus Christ.

In God, Grussendorf says that he has found enough inner peace to meet death face to face. He's had his large intestine removed, had a bone marrow transplant, and just two months ago spent eight days in the St. Mary's Hospital Intensive Care Unit with septicemia, an infection in the blood stream.

"It was pretty touch and go for two days," said Grussendorf, when asked to reflect back on his latest flirt with death. "It's a miracle that I'm sitting here today talking with you."

Grussendorf has run the gamut of emotions over the past four years, when the good health he once took for granted has eluded him.

"If you don't have your health, you don't have anything," he says.

His latest war against death has left the 1963 Hermantown High grad without his old skin on his fingers, hands and feet. He says that new skin is beginning to replace the old, dried up skin. He hopes to be back working at his family business, Grussendorf Nursery, within a month.

"The septicemia disease had nothing to do with the bone marrow problem," Grussendorf said. "It's something anyone can get. The doctors thought I might have to have some of my toes amputated, but as it turned out, everything worked out fine.

"Hundreds and hundreds of people were praying for me."

Grussendorf says that he is willing to accept God's perfect will in his life, and is not afraid of death. "I feel that I'm ready to die," Grussendorf says. "For my own selfish reasons, I'd like to stick around, though. I've got a fantastic wife and four beautiful children that I'd be leaving behind. Going through what I have, I've learned to stop and smell the roses.

"I really believe, though, that God has allowed all of this sickness to give me a good Christian witness. If I can be used to help guide just one person to Jesus Christ, then all of this was worth it."

Grussendorf, the brother of Hawk boy basketball mentor Tom Grussendorf, has been the Esko girls' basketball coach the past five seasons. The Eskomo girls have shared in the highs and lows of their coach's life, and his testimony has left an impact.

"Everyone on this year's team just loves him," said Esko senior Sara Mattinen. "I've never seen people cry so much as when we were at the church praying for him during this last sickness.

"For awhile we were wondering if he would make it. It was hard to believe that we might lose him. I felt it brought the team closer together."

Mattinen says that Grussendorf keeps in touch with the former Esko players and said that she will continue to visit her coach in the years ahead.

"He's taught us much more about life than just basketball skills," said Mattinen, who was a tri-captain in 1984-85. "He always made a point to preach one sermon to us at the start of each season — he tells us about how God has saved his life. He's made the girls think about things like that."

July 1980 · Our Montana Cottage

October 1980 — Leaving Montana and going back home to Minnesota

"Home Sweet Home"

Sharing our faith

Our four girls

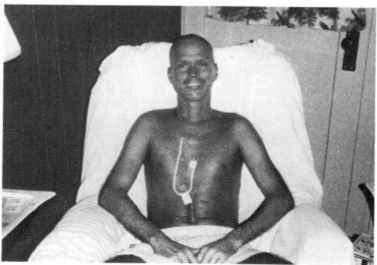

December 1982 — Recuperating following the Bone Marrow Transplant (note: Hickman Catheter)

John Grussendorf Basketball Benefit Night — February 12, 1983

Extending my thanks and appreciation to all

L to R: My dad, brothers Carl and Tom (donor), myself, and brother Jim

Gram and the girls

My wife, Mary, and I

L to R: Our 4 daughters — Miranda, Tanya, Angela, and Brenda

Assistant Coach Bob Swanstrom and myself

Three heads are better than one — myself, Assistant Coach John Bonneville, and Freshman Coach Kathi Munter

My family

"Time Out" for some relaxation

Chapter VII

The Sharing of our Story

Daughters' Thoughts
Miranda (Age 15)

My Dad, John Grussendorf, has been through many trials and tribulations and so have his family and loved ones.

One thing I know for sure is that it is a miracle that my Dad is alive today and I praise God for letting us have him longer here on earth before taking him to Himself in Heaven. The first two episodes about the colitis and the bone marrow transplant I don't know that much about because we were at home and Dad and Mom were at the hospital in Minneapolis. So we really didn't know that much about what was going on.

The septicemia disease is the one that really hit me. Septicemia is an infection of the blood stream. I knew what was going on all the time and I knew it was life-threatening. That's what made me scared. My Dad was so close to dying — I didn't really believe it was true. Maybe it was a dream. I could only wish it was. All anyone could do was pray.

It all started the night before, when he had the chills. The next morning after we had gone to school my Mom said Dad got up and his fingers and toes were turning blue for the lack of oxygen getting to them. They went to Emergency at St. Mary's Hospital and Dad was put into the Intensive Care Unit immediately. The doctor said he was very sick and it was life-threatening. We went to the hospital after school. After some relatives were there and the pastor, we all prayed and after that — things with Dad were stable and the doctor said it was safe to go home. We all thanked God. Weeks later he came home and we all knew it was a miracle.

My Mom was very strong also during this. She stayed with Dad every night he was in the hospital. Our grandma was a big help staying with us while they were there.

We can only thank God for Dad being with us today.

Angela (Age 14)

These past five years have been very special to me. It seems as though I've gotten to know and believe in God a lot more than before. I have more faith in God now that I've seen Him do amazing miracles of healing my Dad. I love my Dad a lot and I'll never forget those sad but yet happy years.

Brenda (Age 13)

My Dad is tough! Let me tell you why. I can't remember very well when he had colitis, but one thing I do remember is he was always in the bathroom. If we were going somewhere we'd sometimes have to stop at a house because he had to go so bad! His next disease — a bone marrow transplant — I remember more. He was away for a *long* time. Gram came to stay with us. I remember when we went to see him in Minneapolis. We went in his room and I started crying because he looked so awful. He didn't have any hair at all! I really don't think I knew how bad those two diseases really were. Finally Mom and Dad came home. I was happy 'cause I had missed them so much.

Then came the septicemia. We went to school and during the day Mom and Dad had gone for a check-up. They weren't there when we got home. Then Gram called and said we were going to the hospital. I think she said everything was okay. But I knew something was wrong when we had to bring some of Dad's things to the hospital. When we got there he was hooked up to all kinds of stuff. He couldn't talk and his hands and feet were blue. He looked really sick. I remember going into the bathroom and going into a stall and crying. I prayed to God to keep him alive. When Pastor Hilman came that got me really scared. I was very *sad*.

But God heard our prayers and saved him for the third time!! I truly believe he wouldn't be here today if *God* hadn't made him better! I was so happy when he got out of intensive care and then came home. I love him and Mom very much. I love God the most — look at all He's done for us!!

Tanya (Age 11)

My Dad is a great Dad!! Sometimes he gets mad at me and almost all the time he is great! I don't know what I can say about him getting sick, but I am glad he is here today. Every time I went by his bed I felt like bursting out in tears but I didn't. I prayed to God every time he got sick. God really does wonderful things. I love my Dad very much! When he was in the hospital all three times my feelings were very down because "why my Dad?" and I felt sad. I love my Dad very, very much and I always will!!!

Dad Grussendorf

"Choose for yourselves whom you will serve, as for me and my house we will serve the Lord." Joshua 24:15.

As John's earthly father, this Scripture has been foremost in my mind since our children were small, and as they grew to adulthood in our family.

I remember when John was only 5 years old when we lived in Kenwood. I had cut down a pine tree, leaving a three foot stump. John had been to church with us many times and when he saw the pine stump he likened it to a pulpit, got behind the stump and started preaching in his childlike language. His words did not come clearly; but in his mind he was proclaiming the Word as a minister would.

John through the years and through his afflictions continued to witness for the Lord. "Many are the afflictions of the righteous — but the Lord delivers him out of them all." Psalms 34:14. How true this has been in John's case. "Suffer hardships with me, as a good soldier of the cross." 2 Timothy 2:3

In spite of his much suffering, John's faith in his Lord has become stronger and I am privileged to be the earthly father of a son who has so much faith.

Mother Grussendorf

Salvation is for all, for the asking and acceptance. Believing all sins forgiven in His name and shed atoning Blood.

Tom Grussendorf

I will never forget the feeling I had the day John called from the hospital. It was about noon when the phone rang at the nursery. John was down in a Minneapolis hospital going through some tests. We were all in the office and getting ready to load the trucks for the next job. The week before, the brothers had our blood tested in case John needed a bone marrow transplant. When I had my blood tested, I didn't think anything would become of it. For one thing, I'd never heard of a bone marrow transplant before and figured John would not need one. For another thing, if it came to a donor, I never thought it would be me. I thought surely Carl, Jim or Eleanore would be better. I was the type of person who gets sick to the stomach just going to visit someone in the hospital.

Well, the phone call on that day was for me. John was on the phone and he sounded pretty jovial. He asked me how would I like to be a donor. At first, I thought he was kidding. Better yet, I hoped to myself he was kidding. I said sure, but down deep I was saying come on John, say you're fooling me. But he never straightened it out. The truth of it is that during that phone call, I got weak and kind of sick. I thought, why me? Here I was, the one that got rubber legs going to visit my wife in the maternity ward, was going to be a donor. On the outside I appeared strong, but on the inside I was shook. I was actually ashamed of my feelings.

After the initial shock, I began to gather my thoughts. Through prayer, the Lord took away these immature feelings. I began to realize how seriously ill John really was. God was going to use my bone marrow to save John's life. That thought sent chills up my spine. What an awesome thought. It wasn't long and I was looking forward to be a part of this miracle.

As far as the transplant operation itself, it wasn't too bad at all for me. I slept during the operation and for about 12 hours after. I really don't remember much. Other than a sore hip for about a week, I felt no physical side effects. Although it was a scary experience, I leaned on the Lord and even in my weakness I was made strong so that the miracle of life could be given to John.

When the surgery was over, we went home and thanked and praised God. Our prayers for John had just begun.

Jim Grussendorf

First Visit after emergency operation to stop bleeding I'll never forget as my brothers and I entered John's room. John looked like a World War II prison inmate, so thin and weak and trying to walk a little for us as if to show us he was doing OK. He could barely stand. We were shocked — trying not to give ourselves away. We were all hurting inside for him, wishing somehow we could share some of this pure misery.

The Long Wait

John slowly but surely recuperates from the Park's procedure operation — all summer he improves — gaining weight — getting his famous suntan back — getting cocky again — kind of getting to be his old self. We all wait patiently for his improvement — and it comes. We even get back into the things brothers will do. Joking, bickering, bartering fishing tackle — it's fun again and we are somewhat relieved — John is back.

Disappointment

After John's long recovery we are disappointed to find John has more serious problems with the onslaught of Aplastic Anemia. We now ask why — why John — he is the strongest spiritually of all of us. Why him? After all he'd been through maybe this isn't too serious — maybe just a short milestone.

Reality

Bone marrow transplant — a new term. This is serious— John will die without it. This is unbelievable — again, why John — the reality of this finally sinks in. We are all disillusioned.

Donor

Who gets to be the donor for John. I know we all hope it will be "me." Maybe we can share just a little of his problems. I was hoping I would be selected — but wasn't.

Fear

I will always remember the prayer meeting at John's house just before his going for the transplant. John was afraid. We were all afraid — this was new to me —never had this dead serious of a problem been experienced before! There we were — all the brothers and the elders of the church. After many had prayed my fear was lessened somewhat. I knew God would answer our prayers — I just knew that John would come through this fearful thing.

Miracle

We've all heard of miracles. Miracle healings that take place from time to time. I pray that one will happen now during this rare and unusual operation. I know it will — remembering the words spoken at the prayer meeting. I'm somewhat comforted during this time as John slowly improves. Hundreds of people praying for John and the miracle healing takes place slowly.

One in a Thousand

Every time we visit we read and enjoy some of the many cards and letters that John and Mary receive. Wonderful notes of support encouraging them to keep the faith and fight just a little bit longer through this long and trying time. Cards from family, friends, his basketball girls, many, many cards. The walls of the room are adorned with them. Mary would pin them up in neat rows. We are amazed at how many Christian friends are concerned for them. Among all these notes of love was one that Mary seemed concerned about. One that was from a friend, but one that would try to cast doubt. A letter that questioned whether our faith was such that healing probably would not take place unless we would now change course, try something new, and deny our life long faith and trust. Amazing how the devil is ever present — even amidst all this genuine Christian love. Upon finding out then that John and Mary's faith was far beyond being impeded by this negative force, I am relieved that their faith increases in spite of this possible stumbling block. Yes, one negative letter in seemingly hundreds got buried and smothered in love and was simply not going to do them in.

Throw in the Towel

Several times during John's long illness he seemed to want to give up. Days turn to weeks — weeks turn to months — months turn to years. A long, long time to be suffering so much. One incident that comes to my mind was when John expressed a desire to "just go home — sit on my deck and die."

Another incident was shortly after the transplant when Graft vs. Host disease made it extremely difficult to eat and swallow. John and I were in his room, he was trying to eat small baby portions of food. The pain was so great that he abruptly stopped, clenched his fists and threatened to throw the plates, food, tray and everything against the wall. The look on his face I shall never forget. He just wanted to call it quits. What's the use, he would say.

Another time he expressed a desire to just get up and walk out of "this prison." "Look, Jim," he said. "The doors are not locked — the cyclone fence around the hospital is open. I could get out very easy."

Painful Departure

After being separated from mom and dad for many weeks, John and Mary's girls finally can have a short visit. A reunion that was long awaited. I recall how the girls wanted to stay with mom and dad. We circled around the hospital entry island several times slowly so the girls could look at mom and wave good-bye . . . a painful departure for all. I'll never forget the sad, solemn looks on the girls faces. It sure was tough to know what to say, dead silence for many miles until I tried to cheer up the atmosphere a little with the promise of possibly stopping at Hinckley A and W on the way back.

Strange Envy

All through the several years of John's illness one experiences unusual thoughts. Thoughts of why so much for just one person. Thoughts of why prayer isn't answered more quickly. Thoughts of how much can John's family endure. Thoughts of — what if John died. How would we handle it? How would Mary and the girls endure it? One very odd thought that I have had from time to time was one of envy. Some strange kind of envy that I had — perhaps I'll never know why. Maybe I wanted to take some of his pain upon myself to somehow lessen his, and I was angered and envious knowing I couldn't. I cannot explain my *strange* envy.

Charity

I have never in my life seen or dreamed it possible to see such faithfulness and dedication from two people. Mary and her mother always remained steadfast —

Mary at John's side for weeks and months away from the girls and Mary's mother at home tending to the needs of the girls. Can you imagine what it would be like for a mother to be away from her children for weeks and weeks? Lonesome for them and at the same time being concerned for a gravely ill husband? And also can you imagine the heartache of Mary's mother, Helen — taking care of the girls — consoling them as required — tending to their everyday needs and at the same time her heart aching for her daughter and John. This unselfish and enduring quality has to be charity. The gift that the Apostle Paul tells us to strive for. The gift that surpasses all other spiritual gifts. The one that is rarely seen. As the weeks and months turned to several years and I continue to observe these two ladies, I can truly say I have seen two people blessed with the elusive gift of *charity.*

Carl Grussendorf

Therefore I tell you, whatever you ask for in prayer, *believe* that you have received it, and it will be yours.
— Mark 11:24

God has performed a modern day miracle in the complete healing of my brother John. It has been quite an experience for me to have actually witnessed a real answering to prayer concerning brother John's battle with septicemia.

I will never forget that long afternoon and evening in February of 1985. I got a call from John's wife Mary to come to the hospital because John was admitted with a life threatening illness. This illness (septicemia) had come very suddenly to John. Within the last several years John has been afflicted with ulcerative colitis and aplastic anemia. God has given many doctors the knowledge and wisdom and through corrective surgery and a bone marrow transplant and many prayers John has overcome these two afflictions and by the healing power of God, has a clean bill of health.

Now, how about this third illness of John's. I asked myself many times why he was afflicted this third time. I'll never forget the gloom and despair as I walked into the hospital's waiting room and met John's wife Mary and my brothers Jim and Tom and our pastor Ray Hilman. As I asked questions to find out how John was and what he had to land in the hospital, I soon found out how serious it was. John had a poisoning of the blood called septicemia. I found out that this disorder can attack anyone no matter how healthy he or she is. For some unknown reason, here John lies in the Intensive Care Unit afflicted for the third time in the last 4 or 5 years.

As we were waiting for periodic doctors reports, we were aware that brother John was in a life threatening situation. We all would comfort one another as we waited for each doctors report. I'll always remember the doctor would say — "John is very ill." "John's *life* is in danger." "The next two hours will be very crucial." "The next two hours we will know if John will make it or not." In these next two hours is where I felt the *Power* of *Prayer* working through everyone.

Pastor Hilman had Jim, Tom and myself together with the pastor join hands and make a circle. We held each other tight as we each took turns asking God for his mercy and for his grace to bring brother John out of this life threatening situation and show signs of improvement. Many tears were shed as we pleaded to God to show his love to John and his family and spare his life *once again*.

During this very same time, unknown to me, my brother-in-law Dave Keippela who was on our church board had called the board and others to gather at the church in Esko to be in constant prayer. Many people were gathered together. Many of John's basketball players and their parents along with members of our own congregation were sending prayers to our Lord and Saviour in John's behalf. I would get a phone call at the hospital from Dave and he wanted to know Johns progress so he could give a report. The first couple of phone calls I remember reporting that John was still in danger and there was no sign of improvement. Johns condition was still going downhill.

Then It Happened! I felt a change within myself. All of a sudden I had a very positive feeling of this whole situation. I could feel God answering all of these prayers. We were waiting for the doctor to check Johns progress again and to give us his report. I'll never forget *waiting* for the doctor to come so we could all go into the Intensive Care Unit. I remember brothers Jim, Tom, sister-in-law Mary, Pastor Hilman, Rod Johnson the Esko basketball (boys) coach and dear friend of Johns, and myself going into Johns room with the doctor. I told the others that this next report was going to be a better one. *I just felt it!* I also remember giving John the thumbs up sign and saying to him, "John this is the report we've been waiting for." The doctor proceeded to check Johns blood pressure, blood count, kidney function, breathing and whatever else they check. The doctors next words were, "all signs have made a *turn* upward," meaning John's body was now working slowly towards *recovery*. From this point John was *not* going downhill anymore. God had taken him and completely turned things around, so we knew he was on the mend. Praise God for answering our prayers. When we returned to the waiting room, we knew John was still very ill but we knew he took a turn for the better and we thanked God and asked God to continue to be with John and his family and bring him through this third trial.

As I am writing this, John has been completely

healed from this septicemia. God has worked through doctors, nurses, family and friends. *God certainly answers prayers.*

John is back working at the nursery this spring, loading and unloading heavy trees and shrubs. We brothers are just amazed at his good health and good attitude, for this is his best spring season he has had since 1981.

Praise God!

Bette Grussendorf

PSALMS 30...Dedicated to John

I will praise you, Lord, for you have saved me from my enemies. You refuse to let them triumph over me. O Lord my God, I pleaded with you, and you gave me my health again. You brought me back from the brink of the grave, from death itself, and here I am alive!

Oh, sing to him you saints of his; give thanks to his holy name. His anger lasts a moment; his favor lasts for life! Weeping may go on all night, but in the morning there is joy.

In my prosperity I said, "This is forever; nothing can stop me now! The Lord has shown me his favor. He has made me steady as a mountain." Then, Lord, you turned your face away from me and cut off your river of blessings. Suddenly my courage was gone; I was terrified and panic-stricken. I cried to you, O Lord, oh, how I pled: "What will you gain, O Lord, from killing me? How can I praise you then to all my friends? How can my dust in the grave speak out and tell the world about your faithfulness? Hear me, Lord; oh, have pity and help me." Then he turned my sorrow into joy! He took away my clothes of mourning and gave me gay and festive garments to rejoice in so that I might sing glad praises to the Lord in-

stead of lying in silence in the grave. O Lord my God, I will keep on thanking you forever!

— from the Living Bible —

One morning when sitting and meditating in my living room, I asked God to help me find a Scripture verse or verses to share with John and Mary. God led me to open my Bible at random to Psalms 30. As I read it God showed me so much through it. He opened my eyes that it truly was a blessing for John.

Later when talking to my sister Sue from Minneapolis that morning and telling her about John's progress, I shared how God laid this Scripture on my heart to share with John and Mary. She mentioned she believed God wants this verse dedicated to John. I read it many times and through John's illness I believed God was going to heal him completely. Later in the afternoon I called John and Mary at the hospital and shared all this with them.

Throughout John's illness my sister, Sue, from Plymouth, kept in contact with me on his progress. Her church, "Vision of Glory," had a constant prayer chain for John.

When Jim and I look back on John's illness we think of all our trips to see John and also Mary. How he suffered so hard and kept hanging in there, and for that God "blessed" John with a miraculous recovery. Then we will never forget "Mary" the pillar of strength that was never ending. She was such an inspiration to everyone. We since have asked her about it. She replied, "I only take one day at a time and thank God for each one. When God picked "Mary" for "John" — He did a perfect job. It was all in His plan.

Gram
What is a Miracle?

In the Scriptures we read of Jesus performing miracles. I believe the main reason for them was to prove to the people that He was the Christ, the Son of the living God. Also, that through His works they would believe as quoted in St. John 10:38. We read how He fed the thousands, walked on the water, made water into wine and had authority over the wind. He healed the epileptic and many others. All these were done by supernatural power. I believe we have seen God's power at work in the healings that have taken place with John.

> What power healed the pouch surgery?
> What caused the bleeding to cease?
> What power made the bone marrow transplant a success?
> What power overcame the septicemia?

The same power that stilled the tempest — that raised Lazarus from the dead — that caused blind eyes to see and the lame to walk!! It was the same resurrection power that raised Christ from the grave! Hallelujah! It is the power of our great Almighty God! "For with God nothing shall be impossible." Luke 1:37

Remembering

I have been amazed at the cross-section of society that was touched by John's illness. Through the calls I received while caring for the girls, I was able to "see" how large and varied was the scope of concerned friends — from local and neighboring communities with added long distance calls! They were neighbors, friends, pastors, students, teachers, college professors, farmers, mill workers, businessmen, truck drivers, etc. It truly shows that through our trials God touches many souls! Each in his own way had a caring heart and a sincere desire to help.

I recall the conversations I had almost daily with the basketball coaches, Mr. Bonneville and Mr. Swanstrom, about the latest hospital reports I had received from

Mary. The Girls Basketball Team, their parents, the coaches, and this vast multitude of friends — we were all as a great family "rooting for the coach."

At times fears and doubts would assail me but I knew I must remain strong for the sake of the girls. It was at these low moments when just contemplating on the love and concern of these numerous friends, offering encouragement and prayers, that I would again be uplifted and refreshed. Through all the trials, the Grussendorf family and I have been sustained by the power of prayer in our behalf. We thank God for all these precious friends who have helped us through difficult times!

How it makes the heart rejoice to see that your children and grandchildren have put their trust in God! When the teachings and values you have tried to communicate and instill, shine forth so bravely in sincere and trusting faith — one can only say, "God of our fathers living still!!"

These girls have grown up in the school of suffering. They know first hand what it is to have sickness in the family. They have been taught and disciplined well — sharing in the chores, doing their homework, etc. But, above all, they were taught early to believe in Jesus and to trust in God. How fortunate that they had this child-like faith to uphold them through these years.

Together we prayed daily for dad's recovery. How often I would see them writing or reciting the "healing passages" from Scripture. Their faith has often been tested by negative reports and repeated hospital stays. What goes on in the mind and heart of a child when there is no sign of a positive answer? *It still goes on believing and trusting!* God has a special protection for children and surely they were upheld by many prayers and the heavenly angels sustained and comforted them!

We have developed a deep bond of love in the years I have taken care of them. I very seldom heard a word of discouragement. Through these trying years they have grown to be beautiful women — and of course, athletes because Dad's the Coach! I'm sure the experience of these years has left them with a greater faith and a trust in God that will carry them through coming years.

Phil Aili

These are some of my thoughts concerning John and Mary and the girls during their plight of the last few years.

First I would like to say that John, my brother-in-law, has always shown such a love and concern for me over the years and has helped me out in many ways a large number of times. He has always been my "big brother" watching out for me and for this I am truly grateful.

Starting way back before John married my sister, Mary, in 1968 when I was just a young lad, John used to always take me grouse hunting or fishing and I so vividly remember that often he used to have to go to the bathroom. He would just say, "You mosey on ahead and I'll catch up to you." When I think back now I wonder if perhaps this was the colitis problem expressing itself already at that time and not simply all the walking in the great fresh air!

Also along those same lines, when I started working for Grussendorf Nursery in 1974, I remember that every day it seemed John would have to hurriedly leave the job scene or make a quick stop at a gas station to go again.

When Mom and I flew out to Montana in 1980 to help John, Mary and the girls move back to Minnesota, I remember observing that John not only looked thin but that he also lacked the ambition to do some of the things I figured we might do out there such as fishing or some serious sight-seeing on our short stay before our drive back to Minnesota. Only then did I realize how sick he really was and how trying it must have been for him to not fully enjoy the Montana life which he so loved and looked forward to. Little did I or any of us realize at that time how much worse or how much harder the days, and months, and years ahead would be.

In the fall of 1982 following John's bone marrow transplant, he developed some complications in the realm of Graft vs. Host disease and I was called upon to urgently drive John and Mary to Minneapolis to see the doctors down there. Being imperative to arrive there as quickly as possible I set the cruise control at 80 mph and let her fly. We were sailing along smoothly until just past Hinckley when I looked in the rear view mirror and saw those flashing red lights. I pulled over and John, who was so sick, jumped out of the car and explained to the officer why we were going so fast. Almost immediately another squad car pulled up. They must have thought they had a real live one going. After taking my driver's license to his car and checking me out, he came back and told us to keep it at 55 mph unless we wanted a police escort or an ambulance. I told him that wasn't necessary and so we proceeded at 55 for about 2 to 3 miles and then I punched it back up to 75 mph or so. Less than a month later the transmission went on my 1980 Monte Carlo with only 27,000 miles. I should have really sent the $360.00 bill for repairs to John.

One of the hardest things for me personally during this whole ordeal was not having John in attendance at my wedding in December of 1982. When my wife, Julie, and I set the date, we had hoped John would have recovered enough from the bone marrow transplant to be able to come but a few complications prevented him from attending. That was so very hard for me and it still hurts when I think of it.

By the fall of 1983, John was feeling so good that he asked me and Julie to help him and Mary on a big landscape job at a racquetball club back out in Hamilton, Montana. Of course we obliged him and it was a most memorable trip and was thoroughly enjoyed by Julie and myself. It was a joy to see John being his old self again and working so hard. Truly the nickname, "Laz," (short for Lazarus whom Jesus raised from the dead) given to him by our nursery crew seemed so appropriate now!

In March of 1985 while working in my fur dressing shop shaving a bear hide on a fleshing machine, this thought suddenly came to my mind, "Oh, if only John could go down state with his girls and win the state tournament before he dies!" Realizing the extent of what I had just thought I offered up a prayer to God on behalf of John, Mary and the girls that God would keep them in His care and if it was in His will that they would in fact go down state. Well 15 minutes later Julie came out into the shop and informed me that my mom had called and said that John was in the hospital. Oh what a feeling that was after just thinking what I had thought. I rushed into the house and called Mom. She told me that John had what the doctors thought at that time was life-threatening pneumonia. She said that he wanted the girls brought down right away in case the worst happened. I hurried to the school to pick up Miranda and Angela who were at basketball practice and I prayed all the way there. I went into the gym and called John Bonneville aside. (He was holding the practice because John had a sore throat.) I told him the situation about John and he was shocked. I went out to wait in the car for Nan (Miranda) and Angie. When they came out I asked them if Bonneville had told them anything and they said no that he was just calling it a short practice. I told them about their dad. The silence and all the emotions and feelings were very hard on a guy. We picked up Mom, Brenda and Tanya and gave the transmission on my new car a workout as we sped to the hospital.

Later that evening when Mom, Mary and I came out of John's room, Mary broke down and said, "He doesn't look very good — does he?" We immediately went to the prayer room adjacent to the waiting room and wept and prayed that God would spare John. It was the same room where the three of us plus the girls would later visit and pour out our hearts once again.

Many hours were spent just waiting and waiting with nothing to do but pray and think. One of the thoughts that perhaps filled everyone's mind at one time or another was this. "What is God trying to tell *me* through all of this?" I know that in my case God was using this latest suffering that John was going through as well as the other times to bring *me personally* into a closer walk with the Lord. He has made me realize my own mortality and to see that this life is so short in relation to eternity. We are like the grass that blooms for awhile and then withers away. God impressed to my heart that this is why it is so important to live for the Lord and serve Him and to tell others about salvation found only through Jesus. "Only one life will soon be past, only what's done for Christ will last." Oh the joy in knowing that when we leave here we can be sure of an eternal home in heaven because of His saving grace! Therefore, I can personally thank God that through all this He has spoken to me and I know He has spoken to many others also. There is no doubt in my mind that it is because of the power of prayer and the love of God that John is still with us today and that He still has a purpose for John in this life. I am so proud to know John who has been counted worthy to suffer like Job and through it all has kept his faith in his Saviour and Lord.

Jim Aili's Letter
Sunday, March 3, 1985

(verse on card)

"Many are the afflictions of the righteous, but the Lord delivereth him out of them all." Psalm 34:19

Dear John and Mary:

Grace, mercy and peace from God our Father and Jesus Christ our Lord.

First it was Job, then Laz, now it's John, because you sure have earned your place among those saints who have suffered for the *Glory of God!*

You have been so close to us in spirit this past week — we have wept with you and rejoiced with you, as I know hundreds have. *Through your suffering* I've come to understand that I don't understand. That has brought *real* peace and also strengthened my faith, not hindered it. I'm just beginning to see now that real faith is not in understanding and comprehending, but in trusting the One who does understand.

We love and admire you (John, Mary and girls) so much and would want to follow your example of real Christian faith and love.

As far as physical healing is concerned, John, you've helped me to realize these things are in our Father's hands.

One small aspect of it has become clearer. . .and that is that *none* of us have perfect health. Perfect health would be to cease to age. We all have the bondage of corruption and are awaiting (future tense) the redemption of our bodies. (Romans 8:18-23)

So dear brother John, be comforted. I'm sorry you have had to suffer so much. But I just want you to know *you've helped so many of us. Thank you!*

I'm so glad Mary got you as her husband; she deserved the best and she got him!

Wanda sends her love and prayers — the children also have been in silence and meditation when you are discussed. I'm sure they are praying in their way. Brother John, you've had to bear a heavy cross. Heaven will reveal all the reasons why. Our prayer is that you would be comforted, for you have comforted us. That you would be strengthened, for you have strengthened us. That you would be healed, for you have been the vessel God has used to heal us. Love and God's Peace! Jim

Pastor Ray Hilman

I count it a special privilege to have been John and Mary Grussendorf's pastor for the last three years. I have been with them through some very bleak and difficult times. These have varied from times in the hospital in Minneapolis, during the bone marrow transplant when it didn't seem like life was worth living, to times of hilarity during our half-time chats at basketball games. Through the gamut of emotions, which they have been allowed to experience, not just once but many times, God's grace and enduring strength have always been real. Their faith in Him as Sovereign Lord has never wavered. Even their own human weaknesses and doubts have resulted in their placing themselves more completely in the hands of their all seeing, all knowing and loving Lord, Jesus Christ.

I do not believe God has punished John by allowing these three major life-threatening experiences. God, in His infinite wisdom, knows and chooses only special people of special character to experience these type of things. When handled properly, it brings glory to God. Others who go through difficulties and suffering are encouraged and strengthened in their faith in God. That God would allow someone to suffer is beyond our human reasoning, but by faith we believe "all things work together for the good of those who love Him, who have been called according to His purpose" (Romans 8:28 NIV). John and Mary have been called, and we praise God for their faithfulness to Him as well as their example to us.

True believers from all around the country, from many backgrounds and ways of life, have been drawn closer to their Lord and closer to each other as they have seen the Lord answer prayers on their behalf.

Of special significance during the most difficult times was the strong support given by both the Grussendorf and Aili families. As a pastor, I have rarely if ever seen such exceptional quality of care-giving. It is great to see true Christianity and true faith in action.

May we all truly praise Him daily for His grace to us all.

Pastor Wayne Juntunen

My first contact with John after he was hospitalized was not a routine pastoral visit. His admittance into the hospital was not routine. Feeling ill he had gone to the doctor for a check-up and was immediately hospitalized. Tests confirmed a serious blood disorder. It was the beginning of a long siege which would take him into the valley of the shadow of death several times.

When a person is seriously ill there is not time for chit-chat. John was more sick than he realized. I saw him several times in the Duluth hospital. He was moved into intensive care. Beginning with my initial visit, prayer was offered for his healing. His condition continued to worsen. The Esko congregation was united in prayer, as were many other congregations and individual believers in various parts of the United States.

John was transferred to the University Hospital in Minneapolis. He was to undergo a bone marrow transplant. One visit which I had with him stands out above all others. In a way which is known only to the Lord Himself, He impressed upon my spirit an over abounding assurance that John was going to be healed. I recalled visiting with John, and sensing a spirit of discouragement within him. But a conviction within me that defied all the visible evidence gave me courage and confidence to speak to John about his healing and pray with full assurance that he was going to make it. I sensed within my spirit that John really believed this was going to be so. In fact I recall he, his wife, Mary, and I were somewhat giddy with an inner joy knowing what was going to transpire.

No, John did not immediately recover. Through many weeks of treatment and several setbacks, he battled against this enemy that wanted to destroy him. But the progress he made encouraged the doctors and his family.

It was a joyous day in early summer to visit John at home after a long winter and spring of almost continuous tension and turmoil. We offered thanks to God for the healing he had experienced, but John was not home free yet. There would be more weeks and months of additional problems and other illnesses not related to the first sickness. Through them all, John was sustained by the grace and power of God. Naturally being human, there were times of discouragement, but the Lord who is faithful in His promise delivered him out of his afflictions.

I thank God for the privilege of being able to be a part of this dramatic episode. Surely John's recovery is a living testimony of the truth of our Saviour's words when he said, "With God all things are possible."

Testimonial Letters From Doctors...

COLON AND RECTAL SURGERY ASSOCIATES, LTD.

EMMANUEL G. BALCOS, M.D.
JOHN G. BULS, M.D.
CARL E. CHRISTENSON, M.D.
CHARLES O. FINNE, III, M.D.
STANLEY M. GOLDBERG, M.D.
FREDERIC D. NEMER, M.D.
DAVID A. ROTHENBERGER, M.D.
JERRY L. SCHOTTLER, M.D.

HOWARD M. FRYKMAN, M.D.
(1917 - 1969)

October 11, 1985

Mr. and Mrs. John A. Grussendorf
190 North Cloquet Road
Esko, Minnesota 55733

Dear John and Mary:

I first met John and Mary Grussendorf on September 25, 1981. John had been sent to me by Dr. Ricard Puumala of Cloquet, Minnesota. John had had a rather severe case of ulcerative colitis for approximately a year and a half and was being greatly inconvenienced by a voluminous number of bowel movements per day as well as having to get up, up to six times per evening. When I first met John, I was impressed with his strength of character, strength of will, but he also had a fear of the disease as well as some mild distrust of physicians, particularly surgeons who might suggest surgery. However, John would not have come to see me, I now know, if he had not, at least in his mind, somewhat come to grips with the possibility of surgery being necessary. There was a vague factor in his history of a possible von Willebrand's disease of prolonged bleeding. There was also the possibility of an enlarged heart. Otherwise, he was in excellent condition. He was a well trained athlete and, of course, did heavy farmwork. My examination initially consisted of a proctoscopy examination which revealed only a mild proctitis. For that reason, I attempted medical management further.

John called me approximately two weeks later with a worsening of his condition. I did a total colonoscopy examination, a review of the entire colon, at which time I found a severe total colonic inflammation. We decided to talk about possible surgery. My recommendation was the new operation to try to retain anal continence and not to have a lifelong ileostomy. This I felt was in John's best interest and would work out best for him as he was well motivated, young, and basically healthy. After some serious discussions, pros, cons, and all possible complications, John's first operation was undertaken at Abbott Northwestern Hospital on December 14, 1981. The operation was difficult but went very well. John was able to be discharged from the hospital in about one week. He returned to Abbott Northwestern Hospital in March of 1982, and takedown of his temporary ileostomy was performed. He initially did well but struggled along with adhesions and a partial obstruction at the anastomosis. This ileostomy construction had to be redone in April of 1982 at Abbott Northwestern Hospital. The patient was doing extremely well and was ready to go home when suddenly for no apparent reason he started to hemorrhage massively from his intestines. He was taken back to surgery where two of my partners explored him, looked for any source of bleeding, and found no exact source of any bleeding. It was then thought that he had a bleeding problem, a coagulation problem, and he was given fresh frozen plasma for approximately one week. The bleeding subsided, and we never found an actual source for the bleeding. Fortunately, after that event, John made an excellent recovery and subsequently to this time has excellent functional control of his anal sphincter and satisfactory bowel pattern.

I believe he will comment that he is pleased with the surgical results. However, several months to a year passed and more trouble was in store for the Grussendorfs. It became apparent that John's bone marrow and blood were failing for some unknown reason. He was seen at the University of Minnesota. Bone marrow transplant, a very dangerous and life-threatening procedure, was recommended and undertaken. Since that time, John has had numerous close calls with death and has come through well. At the time of my dictation of this note, October 9, 1985, John is in excellent health, although he still is at risk because of the immunosuppression he still must maintain because of the bone marrow transplant.

John and Mary have asked me to comment on my relationship with the Grussendorfs over this period of time. I have just given you the medical summary of my relationship with John Grussendorf which just barely scratches the surface of my feelings for John, Mary and their lovely daughters. Since 1981, four years have passed and I have become what I consider to be a friend of the family. And the Grussendorfs are certainly friends of ours. We have eaten together in each of our homes. We have celebrated at meals outside the home and have shared events in each of our families. I feel blessed to know the Grussendorf family because they have been an outstanding and a wonderful example to me of what faith is, what a strong close knit family is, and, for them, what the power of belief, faith and prayer can do. I have met many families in my life with faith in their God but no family have I met with a greater faith than John and Mary Grussendorf. This was particularly impressive to me when John was in the most dire of straits. When near death on a couple of occasions, while very concerned and worried over his own condition, he was able to relax and put his faith in the hands of a greater power. This comforted him and while he was still fearful for his life, he had a peace and the sense of tranquility that only comes from a deep faith, lifelong derived. While I personally do not consider myself a "very religious person," I do not pray daily, my greatest religious belief is in the practice of the golden rule that would be to do unto others as you would have others do unto you. The Grussendorfs practice this, but they practice even more day in and day out belief in their God which has given the family a wonderful strength which has been necessary in their lives in the last few years. My current relationship with the Grussendorfs is mainly one of fun and of a private life as fortunately John has required none of my medical services for the past couple of years. I consider the Grussendorfs to be lifelong friends. I have the utmost respect for them and fondness for them. I look forward to the blessing of many happy family events for us to share with them.

As all of you who know John Grussendorf know, he is a particularly determined individual who, when he sets his mind to it, does not ever accept no for an answer. I think this attitude helped him through those dark moments in his life. Mary Grussendorf comes at life differently — always the gentlest of hearts but strong as a lion within, giving all the faith and backing to her husband that he could possibly pray for. His daughters are exceptional in their upbringing and respect for their parents and their God. I do not mean to reiterate, but just want to stress my feelings of pleasure and privilege to know the family and to have been associated with them during these events.

Sincerely,

Frederic D. Nemer, M.D., F.A.C.S.

FDN:jkw

Enclosures

DC #59-46-97

◗◖ The Duluth Clinic, Ltd.

400 East Third Street
Duluth, MN 55805
218/722-8364

July 29, 1985

Mr. John Grussendorf
190 North Cloquet Road
Esko, MN 55733

Dear John:

My first encounter with John Grussendorf was on September 20, 1982. He was referred by Doctor Philip McGlave at the University of Minnesota Hospitals. His history to that point had been one of ulcerative colitis requiring an ileostomy and colectomy in December, 1981, with an ileorectal re-anastomosis in April 1982. At that time, he had a severe bleeding episode requiring over forty-nine units of blood. In August 1982, he was found to have severe aplastic anemia and was referred to the University of Minnesota Hospitals by his gastroenterologist, Doctor Rick Nemer. Luckily, he was found to have an HLA/MLC compatible brother, Tom. John received total lymphoid radiation on Monday, October 14, and received a bone marrow transplantation from his brother, Tom, on Tuesday, October 5, 1982. My initial contact with him then was in the pre-transplant period, mainly for help with platelet transfusion support. His first blood count at The Duluth Clinic showed a hemoglobin of 10.3, white count of 2000, and a platelet count of 5000.

Following his bone marrow transplantation, during which time he received large doses of radiation and chemotherapy to kill his own immune system, he developed a condition called graft versus host disease which is common in bone marrow transplant patients. This resulted in some significant problems with soreness and ulcers in his mouth, liver dysfunction, a rash and pigmentation of his skin. Although John did not have severe GVH by some standards, this was significantly debilitating and was complicated by the fact that he had a herpes stomatitis which required intravenous Acyclovir therapy in late 1982.

His clinical course, however, continued to improve, he returned to work full-time and, except for some continued difficulty with his bowel function, things were relatively stable until February 25, 1985, when he presented to my office at approximately 4 p.m., having had 24 to 36 hours of fever and chills. He came in severely ill, cyanotic, and in significant distress. At that time, all of his extremities including his fingers, toes, lips, ears, and nose were blue. His blood pressure was 80/60. He was quite lethargic. He was admitted directly from my office to the Medical Intensive Care Unit at St. Mary's Hospital in Duluth, Minnesota, where he was found to be severely acidotic with marked reduction in his kidney function due to a presumed bloodstream infection. The particular bacteria involved at that time could not be cultured as John had taken some Penicillin on the day of admission which made it difficult for us to culture his blood, urine, and sinus drainage, but also may have helped save his life. He was treated with intravenous fluids, corticosteriods, Dopamine, Bicarbonate, and antibiotics. His management was helped by Doctor M.R. Eckman from Infectious Diseases and Doctor R.N. Hellman from Nephrology. He had a severe pharyngitis (sore throat), and it became apparent that he had a significant infection in his sinuses, which we felt was probably the area where the bloodstream infection began. He later developed gangrene of his nasal septum and several of the digits on his toes which, because of his previous vigorous health and excellent circulation, he was able to heal essentially completely.

This, of course, is a skimpy outline of the significant distress, numerous tests, medications, and concern that have gone into John's day-to-day and week-to-week medical care and quality of life since early 1982. Many more pages could be written outlining these important events, but there are more important things that participating in John's care mean to me as one of his physicians.

The first thing that is apparent in the doctor/patient relationship with John Grussendorf is that one deals with him "straight on." He likes to hear it as it is. To me, this has been one of the real pleasures in dealing with him as a patient and has certainly made the numerous difficulties easier to manage.

Second is the fact that the Grussendorf family has a sterling reputation in Northeastern Minnesota as being excellent (in fact, the best) nurserymen. Because this is how he functions in his work life, he also expects this of the physicians and paramedical people who participate in his care.

Thirdly, John was the first bone marrow transplant patient whose care I was involved in. Since then, there have been several more, but medically this was a new experience for me. Graft versus host disease, a unique problem with bone marrow transplant patients, was a new disease entity for me to learn about and help manage. It also opened doors of further fruitful association with Doctor Philip McGlave, the head of the Adult Bone Marrow Transplant Unit at the University of Minnesota

Hospitals, with whom I have subsequently had a fruitful and rewarding relationship, both with John and other patients. It is apparent to me that everyone who has been and is involved in John's care gets emotionally invested with him because of the kind of individual he is.

Fourthly, I have had the pleasure of some contact with the Grussendorf family. In a day and age when divorce rates are high and family life is suffering, this is a family with old-fashioned values which include mutual help and aid in times of trouble for each other. To a physician whose practice includes many patients with malignant and other serious diseases, the strength derived from religious faith and friend and family support cannot be over-emphasized as a contributing factor to the hope and courage required in times of crisis. These relationships do not develop at a time of crisis alone. In a family like the Grussendorf family, they have to be there, in place all the time, only to be called upon when needed and cannot be "drummed up" in the hour of need.

I know that John and his family rely heavily on their religious faith for strength. When one sees a patient as sick as John with a non-functioning vital body organ such as the bone marrow, later completely recover through the help of his family and medical science, it is almost like getting a small glimpse of the resurrection. That thought has crossed my mind many times as I see him now back as a strong and self-reliant individual. Revelation 21:5 comes to mind, "And He sat upon the throne and said, Behold, I make all things new."

Your physician and friend,

Robert D. Niedringhaus, M.D.

RDN/dcb

D.C. #59 46 97

▶◀ The Duluth Clinic, Ltd.

400 East Third Street
Duluth, MN 55805
218/722-8364

July 24, 1985

Mr. John Grussendorf
190 No. Cloquet Road
Esko, MN 55733

Dear John:

This is the story of my relationship with John Grussendorf. I first met John in the first of March of 1985 while he was in the hospital. He was in the Intensive Care Unit. His fingers and toes were purple; he was extremely weak, and all in all I did not see that there was much life in this man. Having never seen John before, I truly felt that he was not long destined for this world.

John had been hospitalized on 2/25/85 with a 24-hour history of fevers, chills, and general sense of ill-being. This progressed rapidly to a condition of septic shock. This is essentially a total body infection which results in the drop of blood pressure and a total body collapse. Because of this he developed blue fingers and toes, some of which developed gangrene from the incident. In addition, part of his nose developed gangrene. After some investigation it was thought that this problem had started with a sinus infection and that was the reason for my consultation.

As mentioned above, John was in tough shape when I first saw him; because of his situation his spirits were down and his pain tolerance was quite low. On several occasions we tried to clean his nose from all of the gangrene but finally on March 6 he was taken to the operating room, where, under general anesthesia his nose was cleaned out and his sinuses washed. Because of the serious condition, surgery had to be hurried and even at that time there were some real doubts as to whether John would be able to recuperate. However, after surgery he gradually improved and by the 10th of March he was able to go home.

Through this time I became aware of John's past medical problems. His chart reads like a textbook of medicine. I will not detail all of the various medical problems that John has had to struggle with, only to mention that many patients have succumbed to any one of the many problems that John has been able to overcome.

During those days after surgery John's strength slowly returned. After discharge I saw John on many occasions to clean his nose and sinuses and also had the opportunity to get to know he and his wife better. After many visits to the office it became apparent that John would need further surgery on his nose and sinuses. John had had previous operations done at the University of Minnesota and we discussed that he should probably return to the University to have this sinus surgery performed. However, it was gratifying for me that John placed his trust in my medical ability and insisted that I perform his surgery.

On 3/27/85 John went back to the operating room where more extensive nasal and sinus surgery was performed to provide a more definitive solution to his ongoing nasal and sinus problems. Fortunately, everything turned out quite well and at this time it appears that John has once again overcome another major medical stumbling block.

Throughout these months as I have interacted with John and his family, it has become clear to me that it is no coincidence that John has been able to overcome all of the medical challenges that he has faced. John is a hard charging man full of energy and inner strength. These qualities are shared by his wife and also seem to percolate throughout the family.

It has been a pleasure and an inspiration for me to participate in John's medical care as well as the opportunity to get to know him as a fine person.

Your friend,

William Portilla, M.D.

WP:klr

We wish to express our thanks and appreciation to the medical profession — the doctors, the nursing personnel, those in research and all who have dedicated their lives to help the suffering and afflicted. With their knowledge, skilled care and loving concern, theirs is truly a great labor of love. Together with God's healing power they can perform miracles. May they be rewarded by knowing their work is truly needed and gratefully appreciated by the families going through sickness and suffering.

We pray for progress in the field of medicine. May God give wisdom as they ever seek to find new cures for the threatening diseases of today. We thank the numerous others who have allowed themselves to be tested so that research may progress. The world owes much to them.

The Grussendorfs

Bob Swanstrom

My basketball coaching relationship with John started in the summer of 1979, when I wrote him a letter "out of the blue" informing him of the vacancy at Esko for A and B squad girls' basketball coaches for the coming season. John, Mary and the girls were living in Hamilton, Montana at the time. John mentioned later that the family was looking for a sign to return home. Unknown to me, John was in the throes of his colon inflammation. As I look back five years later, maybe that letter played a significant role in the course of John's life, and just how his life has in turn affected *so many lives* including my own. One does things in the course of one's life never fully realizing the impact it may have on others. We impact each other in so many ways by just being in contact.

Our first basketball season together was a real *learning* and *growing* experience for both of us. John quickly learned that coaching girls' basketball was far different than what he remembered boys' basketball to be. Early drubbings by area powers Duluth Central and Moose Lake brought out more than a few "Coaches' Nightmare" comments by John. The girls didn't have the fundamentals John was used to and they didn't progress as quickly as he desired. John considered quitting out loud a few times to me. To his credit, he didn't and instead slowly developed the girls into a respectable team. As a point of interest, my "B Team" was undefeated after 4 games and I was riding high. John's "A Team" was 1-3 at the same time. Our fifth game was at Hermantown, both our alma maters, and my whole family turned out to see the game. John informed me shortly before game time that he was taking my two starting guards — both of them 9th graders — to play on his "A Team." My undefeated B Team got smoked and *was I ticked!* John's A Team won that night. The Old Stag just couldn't let the Young Buck get too far ahead of him.

I learned a tremendous amount about coaching from John that first year together. The girls kept improving steadily, due mostly to John's coaching and their dedication to be winners. They were in there plugging to the best of their abilities. John's voice was a prime candidate for Northwestern Bell's "Reach Out and Touch Someone" Award. He believed in "coaching constantly" as the game was in progress. He was always vocalizing to his charges, and roaming the sidelines with much intensity and emotion. I threatened to tie a string to his belt loops to reel him in every time he strayed too far. He didn't cotton to be a "human yo-yo." When he did stay on the bench, he'd continually elbow me or knee me whenever he got excited, which was often. You talk about black and blue — I was considering applying for combat pay!

We ended the first season playing our very best game against power Silver Bay losing by 1 point, 41-40. Progress had been made and we were already looking forward to the summer basketball season, and then into next fall.

John instituted a very *well attended* basketball program during the summer months. For the girls it was just like another season. John's dream of having his girls play the game of basketball like the boys do was well on its way to materializing. Kim Juntunen played a major part in the summer programs.

During our second year, John decided to go with our younger players to throw them into the fire so to speak. The Lani's, Eli's, and Lori's developed during the course of the season into quality ballplayers. John and I grew closer as coaches and things really shaped up with the girls' basketball program. At Christmas time, John had his colon removed. I took over as interim head coach for 4 weeks until he returned. The second season ended in the district semi-finals with a poor performance against Morgan Park.

In late spring John was back in the hospital again with extreme internal bleeding. He survived after numerous close calls! Brother Carl and I spearheaded a drive to get 56 blood donors to replenish what John had needed. Athletic Director, Julian Bertogliat, was a tremendous help in this effort by getting 32 donors by himself.

John mentioned to me that he was going to have a bone marrow transplant in the fall just before basketball season was to start. I had just lost my teaching job at Esko and he asked if I'd step in as interim head coach along with John Bonneville as my assistant. I agreed to head up the team not knowing how long it would be until John returned. As it was it ended up being three months.

I was glad to be in a position to help John particularly, and the girls generally, as the head coach. To be honest, there were a number of factors that made those three months very difficult for me. I endured with constant support from Bonneville and a lot of phone calls to John. We started slowly, but each game we improved and played together as a team within our abilities. We lost our first game to Duluth Central, and then started on a 20 game unbeaten streak. My highlight was the Cromwell game. John had to turn off the radio late in the game because he couldn't stand it anymore. We hung in there to win an extremely close game. The total team really came together that night and played their finest ball game. *We won it for John!* That game was my fondest moment. John returned the following week to a team that was 12-1 and he guided them to a District 26 Championship, and into the Regions. We lost our first regional game to powerhouse Chisholm ending the season with a record of 20-2. Most of the girls were juniors so John had much to look forward to the following fall.

I bowed out after that third season together. John Bonneville stayed on continuing to assist John as "B Squad" coach. They were an ideal two-some to coach the girls.

That fourth season I watched frequently from the stands. John and the talented team fared very well together. They won the Wood City Classic, won the Polar League Title, the District 26 Title, and played in the Region 7 Tournament for the second time. I compiled a scrapbook for John that included all the newspaper clippings, programs, etc., that sequentially detailed their very successful basketball season. It meant a lot to me to put this scrapbook together for him and give it to John as a gift from the heart.

This past season, with most of his horses graduated or moved away, John had a real coaching job on his hands. Toward the end of the season, the team matured to the point where they knocked off some real powers in the area — Cromwell, Northwestern, Moose Lake, etc. During the course of the season, John would call me after big victories to share the big news. I'm glad he had another close friend to share his thoughts, emotions, and excitement with — I'm glad I was that special friend who he could call and who could understand and relate exactly to what he was saying. I really enjoyed our phone conversations very much!

A highlight for me was sending John six red roses on the eve of the District Basketball Tournament. It was right after the big Moose Lake victory. John has adopted a favorite saying of mine, "Don't walk so fast that you can't smell the flowers." The roses were sent with sensitivity to help him smell the flowers. Little did I know that three days later John would be back in the hospital near death with a blood infection. Bonneville took over the team and the girls played admirably! After many trying days, John pulled through.

In a phone conversation later, we discussed writing a book. He asked for my reflections which I've written down on these pages.

One last parting reflection that I observed and one that was an evident underlying force in John's whole story is the following observation. Throughout John's health ordeal, the support he received from his wife, Mary, his 4 daughters, his extended family, Grandma Aili, church congregation, friends, athletes, etc. was something for me to behold. The steadfast devotion of Mary to constantly be at John's bedside is a *story in itself!* She is truly a remarkable woman. Grandma Aili moving in at a moments notice to keep stability with the girls was something special. Many a time Grandma and I talked on the phone about John's current situation. She's a *true mother* in every sense of the word. The four girls held up remarkably well throughout the whole experience.

You have to be extremely proud of your "Golden Girls." The Grussendorf brothers and sister along with the Aili brothers were always close by — ready to show support and encouragement when needed.

Grandpa Deke and Mumu were on top of things always. The "ripple effect" of church members, neighbors, coaches, athletes, teachers, news media, etc. was very gratifying for me to witness. The "John Grussendorf Benefit Basketball Game" was a tremendous tribute by all these people who John and his family had touched, who in turn touched the Grussendorfs with their attendance and contributions on that memorable night. I'll never forget that very special evening!

John Bonneville

Things seemed to start several weeks before John and Mary moved to Montana. I remember John telling me how he had diarrhea all the time! We laughed about it and blamed it on nerves. You had to know that John was hyper about going out and starting a business, renting out his house and furnishings and leaving the cattle and farm in my hands. That probably made him the most hyper of all!

I remember phone calls from Montana, John always had a list of things for me to check on or do — snow on house — light on in pump house if it gets too cold — always remember to drain water line in barn — chop ice in bathtub for cattle to drink rather than run tank heater and use up electricity — snow off of lean-to — chop ice around barn door so water won't run into barn in the spring — move old hay to one side — put new hay in the middle — leave room for conveyor to go out — don't put wet bales in with good hay — feed old hay first so they had good stuff during winter

— check and cut around fence line — watch for calves being born — deposit rent in checking account — etc. After taking notes, then John would tell me how they loved it out in the Bitterroot Mountains. Even though things were going good, John was still having problems with diarrhea and was having it checked out at a hospital there.

I remember him telling me on the phone that he had some kind of colitis and that through medication and by watching his diet that it could probably be controlled.

I wanted John to coach boys basketball again with me. This would be a good group of boys and a "last hurrah" for us both but it didn't work out that way.

Coming home — probably a time of mixed emotions. They had a great time out there and made some wonderful friends. They had worked as a family and had a successful business. John became involved with long bow hunting and that is all he talked about — hunting deer and bear with a long bow.

John had a new challenge of coaching *girls* basketball at Esko. As the season went along that winter, John would call me up after a ball game and tell me they turned the ball over 25 times that game! They shot 15%!! What a change from coaching boys! He hung in there and made it through his first year of coaching girls.

Things weren't getting any better with the colitis. In fact, it was getting a lot worse. Work started that spring at the nursery and that summer was very hard for him. John was up 6 to 8 times during the night to go to the bathroom. Working hard and not getting enough rest was taking a toll on him, physically as well as mentally.

I can remember many times riding along in the car or truck with John and having to stop for him to go into a bathroom. One time coming along the Erickson Road, I stopped and John ran into the woods. A very frustrating time for him. It didn't look like medication was going to solve the problem for him either. John had given up eating some things that would increase the diarrhea and still the colitis was getting worse instead of better.

From the very start of John's physical problems, he asked that we pray for his healing. We prayed for John in our daily lives and also had church members pray for him. Even with prayer, John's condition was getting worse instead of better. I remember praying for John and asking for the Lord to work things out for him, the way the Lord would have it to be! We sometimes pray for the Lord to work things out the way *we* want them worked out. Looking back now, the Lord had much more for John to go through.

The fall of 1981 was the first time that John didn't come up to the hunting shack with us for deer season. Things were going downhill for him and going fast.

I remember how John kept talking about how rotten life would be if he had to solve this colitis problem with an external bag. No playing ball — working with his shirt off — no beach — Why me?

John heard about a new operation that could be done on certain patients that had colitis. This new operation would have an internal pouch instead of an external pouch. Once this was done, a person would be as normal as anyone else. He went to Minneapolis to talk to the doctor that performs this operation. John was the type of patient that could have this internal pouch. Even though this was an option for John, he still felt that the Lord would heal him without having the operation.

Things continued to get worse for him. Basketball was going strong now and John was having more problems with his colitis. Finally in December of 1981, he decided to have the operation. He would miss just one ball game before being back into coaching. (I guess that is why it helps to be nuts to be a head coach. John plans this major operation around his basketball schedule so he won't miss many games!)

John was very happy about this operation because he would have no external bag and would be normal in every way. He had to have the external bag for several months while everything healed inside.

The time went fast and in March, John went down to have the external bag removed and everything hooked up inside. The operation went great and he was home soon. He seemed very happy that the operation was over and that he could be back to normal again.

John was home for less than a week when he was experiencing some bad pains and he went back down to Minneapolis to the hospital. Internal bleeding! Another operation to correct the problem. That operation almost cost John his life. Doctors couldn't find where the bleeding was coming from but the Lord stopped the bleeding and John came home.

That summer was very difficult for him. His weight was down and he was very tired. He had a broken water line out in the barn one day. John and I had to pull the plastic pipe apart and replace a piece. Normally that wouldn't have been a very big job but John was unable to put much effort into it for fear of hurting himself. Another one of many frustrations that John was going to have.

Even though the new pouch was working fine, John still had to get up many times during the night to go to the bathroom. Doctors told him that the medication, diet and time would solve that problem. Still the broken sleep at night was difficult and John was very tired trying to work full time.

That August, John had some blood work done in Minneapolis and he found out that he had "Aplastic Anemia." I remember him telling me that it was a very rare blood disease where the bone marrow just quits working. Dejected, John said the chances of surviving this disease weren't very good! Why me?

Again prayers went out for him. Hundreds of people were praying that the Lord would heal him and save him from going through a lot of pain and suffering but again the Lord had other plans for John's life.

Time went on and it was decided that John was going to have a bone marrow transplant and that his brother, Tom, would be the donor. John knew that before he could receive Tom's bone marrow, all of his bone marrow would have to be killed through radiation and along with the radiation would come much pain, suffering and side effects. Not a pleasant experience to look forward to but he had no other choice.

I can remember standing with John out in his driveway one day before the transplant. The doctors said his recovery time after the transplant would be about six weeks. John asked me if I would consider helping Bob Swanstrom coach the girls basketball team until he could continue again. John figured that by the time Christmas vacation was over, he should be back coaching. I told him 'no problem' — I would do anything to help out. Little did I realize that I would spend three seasons coaching girls basketball.

Before John left for Minneapolis and the bone marrow transplant, we had several talks about the soon to be basketball season and what my part would be. John had a long list of things I had to be aware of and how I was to react in certain situations. He wanted me to be the one to holler and be the mean one while he was gone. He was worried that we wouldn't push the girls as hard as he had done and they would become a regular girls basketball team instead of the "Run and Gun," full court man to man — get on your guy type team that John had and still wanted. John constantly kept telling me how *tough* I had to be on them. I assured him that I would be 'tough.'

John had the bone marrow transplant and now was in a long recovery period. This was also the beginning of many, many phone calls to John's mother-in-law, Mrs. Aili, who was taking care of his kids while Mary was in Minneapolis with him. We would talk almost every night about how things were going with John's progress.

One day while talking to one of his brothers, it was mentioned that the three brothers were planning to go down and visit John on a Thursday. Maybe a visit would cheer him up a bit and help him pass the time. The idea of going down to visit John sounded great and I offered to go along. I could take a personal day of leave from school to go with. That sounded good until the next day when Carl called and in a polite-tactful way, said that it was just going to be the three brothers going down. That Thursday was to be called "Black Thursday" for me. I really had hoped to go down and see John — but it was not to be.

The recovery period after the transplant was also the time for the hundreds of reports that I would be giving to the many people that would ask about John's condition. No matter where I was — someone wanted to know how he was doing. Sometimes I wished I had a tape recorder to play a taped report instead of going over the report again and again.

It wasn't long after the transplant that the lab reports started to show that the bone marrow was starting to work. In fact, it was amazing how fast the recovery process was going. John was out of the hospital in 28 days. This was the fastest that any transplant patient had gotten out. Our prayers were being answered!

During this hospital stay and the week or so that John stayed at his sister's house in Minneapolis, we learned about the term Graft versus Host disease. John's body was going to try and reject this foreign substance and in so doing, he would be exposed to many side effects.

Probably the most painful and longest lasting of all the side effects that John would have was the cold sores in his mouth and throat. These sores caused so much pain that swallowing became almost unbearable. John's weight started to drop rapidly. I can remember several times talking to him on the phone from the hospital and later on when he stayed at his sisters. These talks were usually very depressing. It seemed his conditions would be *"one step forward and two steps backwards."* John was even down on basketball! Basketball had always been a positive driving force for him. It was another reason to fight this disease that he had. The fight for basketball was beginning to fall by the wayside.

I remember one of those talks with John that left me feeling totally depressed and in tears. He was down on life that night and he told me that if he knew then what he knew now, he would have never had the transplant. The pain and side effects just weren't worth it! He would have been better off just letting the disease take its course and hope that prayer would cure it. Needless to say, anything I tried to say to cheer him up or become positive, just didn't work.

Maybe it was the frustration that had built up inside me, or the total feeling of helplessness that I had, my best friend going through all this pain and suffering and there was nothing I could do or say to help ease the pain. Whatever it was, I had to get it off my chest. I had some very *strong* words for John that night. I told him he was feeling sorry for himself, was starting to sound like a quitter and not the fighter that he really was and that we were suffering along with him in our own way! I was sitting on the floor leaning against the wall telling these things to John that night. After we were through, I sat there telling my wife that I felt like a huge weight had just been lifted from me but how badly I felt because of the things I had just said. How could I say those things to a man that was becoming a modern day Job?

For the next few days I had a very empty feeling in my stomach concerning my talk with John. I kept telling myself that I had to tell him how I felt and I hoped that he would understand. Well I got a phone call from John shortly after. He was still in a lot of pain but he was *very* positive! What a change in his attitude from just a few short days before! John was back to being a fighter again instead of a quitter.

I can remember when John got to come home. We were told that he didn't want to have any visitors at all. I talked to him on the phone a few times and then one day he asked me to come over. This would be the first time I had seen him since before going down for the transplant. I walked in the door and stood waiting for John in the kitchen. Soon he came into the room and stood looking down at the floor. He wore a pair of sweat pants, t-shirt and stocking cap. He was nothing but skin and bones except for his face, that was very swollen with lips that had many sores on them. John's skin was even discolored. I remember him reaching up and removing his stocking cap and then looking at me and saying, "Pretty sad, hey Bon?" Yah, it wasn't the best looking body I've seen but it was John and he was *alive!!*

Seeing John like that was really tough. I never expected to see him looking that bad — but he did! I knew it was going to be a while before John would be back coaching full strength but that didn't bother me. The only thing that mattered was that he got better each day.

Our first visit was pretty short. John was very tired and on lots of medication so he needed lots of rest. Even though it wasn't long, at least John had broken the ice with me as far as his looks were concerned. Now we could get down to other things.

Before the season started, I had hours and hours of conversations with Bob Swanstrom and John concerning the basketball team. We talked about how practices were going to be — what drills to use — how many sprints to run — what kind of offense and defense to use and even what rules we would have and the consequences if any rule was broken. Many times my wife would remark that I spent more time talking to them than I did with her and she was right.

The season finally started and I had my first encounter with coaching girls basketball. After watching the girls practice, I could see why John enjoyed coaching girls basketball. They were full of enthusiasm, had lots of speed and talent and they loved to play the game. The ingredients for an excellent team were there, now it was a matter of getting them to perform as well for us as they would for John if he was there each day.

I remember the first day John came to practice. This was the first time that the girls had seen him since the bone marrow transplant except for a few of the starters. John and I had talked about how he was going to show up for practice for that first time. We decided to keep everything on the light side and not be serious about his looks. When John came into the gym, I made the comment how he looked like a cue ball on a pair of stilts. We all laughed together and the ice was broken concerning his looks.

I look back at the many times that John showed up at practice to watch for awhile. He always gave the appearance that things were going good when really he must have been hurting inside. Just talking to the girls in a soft voice would cause John extreme pain. His visits would always inspire the girls and they would always work harder when the "Coach" was there. John would call players over and tell them to work harder or to get the team going because he felt they were loafing a little. He always told the girls that we were in charge and they were to do what we said until he was able to come back and coach again.

John's visits to practice always seemed to give the team a lift but I think they were probably bad for his recovery. Many times he would 'over-do-it' and be real tired the next day. He probably should have just stayed home and rested his weak body but that was just impossible for a guy that had his brother's bone marrow in his body and basketball in his blood.

John just *had* to be near *his* team.

The days turned into weeks and weeks into months. The team was having a great season and John's recovery was going good. Somewhere towards the last quarter of the season he decided to come back to coaching the team again. We were all happy to hear that he was going to be back. Now I could become a retired coach again and have more time to devote to my wife and two sons. But... John told me that he would only return if I stayed on coaching too! So much for becoming a spectator!

We finished the season with the three of us coaching. We all had something different to contribute to the team. At practice John would sit in his swivel chair with rollers and coach the team. I sometimes wonder how many miles that chair has on it from going back and forth along the sideline as he coached.

John still had problems with his throat and talking too loud or just plain yelling wasn't good for it! When one of the girls needed to be spoken to, he would have her run over to him where he could talk to her in a normal tone of voice. He even used a battery powered bullhorn to give instructions to the team during practice.

Sometimes before a ball game John had to take his medicine that he needed. He would usually tell me to keep an eye on him because he felt lightheaded from the medication. Many times during games I had to tell him to relax and not yell so much. Just another one of the many side effects of the medication that he had to take.

Through all the trials and tribulations, we managed to make it through the season. The girls won the conference title, the District 26 title and then were beaten in the semi-finals for the Region 7 title. They ended up with a 20-2 record.

So the end came to my first season ever of coaching girls basketball. It was a very trying but yet rewarding season. I'm just glad that John was back coaching again when the season ended.

That summer John learned that Bob Swanstrom would not be able to be the assistant coach for the coming season. Bob had taken a new job and would not be able to coach again. John asked me to think about the possibility of me coaching again. He just wanted me to think about it over the summer and let him know at the end of August. After talking it over with my wife, I decided to coach again with John.

The 1983-84 season was quite a change from the season before. John's health was very good compared with the season before. Now that he was back in full strength, the girls worked much harder than they did the year before. We were fortunate to have another group of fine athletes and again when the season ended, the Esko girls had won another Polar League Championship, District 26 title and were beaten in the semi-finals of the Region 7 play.

The 1984-85 season began on a good note. John was feeling very good. Although he still had to take various kinds of medication, he felt and looked very good.

This was going to be a rebuilding year for the team. John worked the girls very hard at practice. Lots of running and a very tough defense.

John was really enjoying this season. For the first

time in several years, he felt real good. His weight was back and he felt much stronger. Things just seemed to finally fall into place.

John was very positive about everything. In fact, if I could catch him complaining about life, I would get $100.00. I would purposely come to practice and complain about the weather, or how I felt etc., and John would always laugh and say "it's great to be alive!" He was always looking at the positive side of things and for sure he was taking time to smell the roses! I never did win that $100.00 from him and I'm glad!

We had another good season. We won some games that people thought we'd lose and lost some that we could have won. John's health was good except for a sore throat or cold now and then.

We were playing real well towards the end of the season. With a few breaks we felt that our team could win the District 26 title again.

The district tournament started and we played on a Saturday afternoon. We won that game and John and I were just enjoying the other games that were being played. Our team had to play again on Tuesday night. Monday, around noon, I got a call from John that I had to take practice by myself because he had to go to the doctor at 4 p.m. He sounded like he had a bad sore throat. I thought he was just kidding me and I laughed and said "You bet!" John assured me it wasn't a joke and he really did have to go at 4 p.m. We discussed what to go over that night and we said good-bye.

Things were going fine that night at practice. The girls were looking very good and we felt we had a good chance to win our next tournament game around 5 p.m. John's brother-in-law, Phil, came into practice. He called me over and said John was in intensive care and things didn't look good for him. I stood there speechless — was this another "bad dream" I was having or what? Phil said they weren't sure what was wrong — he may have some fast acting pneumonia or something. Phil had been told to stop at practice and pick up John's two daughters and bring them down to the hospital.

I finished practice as usual — but then I had the girls sit down so I could talk to them. After telling them what time the bus would leave and what color uniforms we would wear for the game on Tuesday, I told them about their coach. Most of these girls had been through three years of sickness with John. They asked questions that I didn't have answers to. I didn't even know much about what had happened. The one thing I did know was that John was going to need their prayers. So on that note we left the gym.

Later that night, we got to the waiting room hoping for some good news on John's condition and some answers to our many questions. I can remember coming into that area and seeing all the family and friends sitting there with very, very sad faces!! I didn't like what I saw and I began to wonder if my best friend was going to live this time. I never had that fear with all the other problems John went through. I always knew he was going to recover and be himself again. But this time no one knew what was causing this problem and there wasn't much time left. Either something had to turn things around soon or John was gone.

Members of John's church had been called and prayers for him had begun. Friends from other churches were called and prayer chains were started. Late that evening we were told that John's condition was on hold. The infection seemed to have stopped and he seemed to be holding his own. The doctor told us to go home and the next 24 hours would be very critical for him. Before we left, Pastor Hilman had a word of prayer with us.

The next day seemed to drag on forever. There didn't seem to be any real change in his condition, just a "wait and see" attitude.

That night at practice things just didn't seem to make sense. We were there going through the motions but yet we were with John down in the intensive care unit. We talked about any new news someone might have and reminded everyone to say a special prayer for him again that night.

After practice we went down to visit John. This time I got to visit with him. I felt uneasy going into his room. Thoughts about him not making it through this one left me with a lump in my throat. When I saw him, you just knew he was very sick. I couldn't understand how he could have gotten so sick in such a short time but he did. Once again John was fighting for his life.

Somehow throughout that week we managed to play two more ball games. I remember calling the hospital for a report on John before and after the games. So many people came up and asked about his condition. Once again, over and over I would repeat what happened to John and how he was doing.

Our season ended that week but for all practical purposes, it ended on Monday when John went into the hospital. Our thoughts and prayers were with him that week and somehow playing basketball just didn't mean a whole lot.

Before each ball game, John or I would usually have a word of prayer with the team. We have tried to impress upon the girls that there is more to life than basketball. We have to enjoy each day to its fullest. Each day has so much to offer to us and somehow we go through the day with blinders on. I think we all learned to appreciate our lives a lot more.

The Bible tells us that the Lord will never put you through more trials and tribulations than you can handle. Also, we are told that some things that happen on earth we will never understand but someday in heaven, we will. I quit trying to figure out why John and his family have gone through so much but I'm sure when he stands before the throne of Glory, he will hear "Well done my good and faithful servant."

Marie Bonneville

Special people and special friends — that is what John and Mary Grussendorf are. Our friendship, as two couples, started growing around the time of our marriages. Over the years, our friendship has grown stronger and we have shared many special times together. We have shared good times and bad times, laughter and tears. Very special times include celebrating anniversaries, dinners out and many New Year's Eves together. They have become a tradition. Instead of going out on the town, we find enjoyment in a quiet evening at home with pizza, pop, games and sometimes a sauna. One memorable evening was a candlelight dinner at our home. We kidded John that he had to dress appropriately for the occasion and not wear his traditional sweat pants. When he arrived, he was wearing the pants from his wedding suit as well as the jacket. They were a little snug as well as high water. We all had a good laugh and he was changed into more casual clothes within minutes.

In 1980, when John and Mary decided to go to Montana, we had mixed emotions. We felt excitement for them in the adventures that would lie before them but we felt a sadness too in seeing them go. On the day of their departure they stopped over early in the morning for coffee, cocoa and rolls. We experienced an empty feeling as we watched them drive away. They elected us to be 'landlords' of their farm property while they would be away. What a disaster! The renters were a nice young couple so there were no real problems with them. The beef cattle were another story!

Shortly before Grussendorfs left for out west, a calf was born that was deserted by its mother. Grussendorfs took special care of this little calf. When John Grussendorf discovered it, it was covered with frost and almost lifeless. He brought it down into their basement where they gave it lots of TLC and even used a hair dryer to warm it and thaw it out. Life returned to it. They named this calf "Frosty," a very appropriate name due to the circumstances surrounding its birth. We had problems with other calves also. Often the mother would desert her newborn shortly after birth so we had a lot of coaxing to do. We didn't lose any newborns, but suffered some frustration during those births. It was a totally new experience for our family. When the muddy season ended and the grass started growing, the animals were put out to pasture. That is when our troubles really began. Due to drought conditions, the grazing pasture was terrible. It was enclosed by an electric fence. Outside of that electric fence was our hay field which was growing much better. The cattle weren't going to let a little electric fence stand between them and better grazing. The calves were able to get under it and the bigger animals found ways out also. Our telephone was ringing quite often with neighbors on the other end informing us that one or more cows were out — then the chase would begin. One evening after 10 p.m. we had a knock on our door. It was a neighbor telling us that one of our calves had been struck by a truck and killed on the highway. It was Frosty. We hated to tell John and Mary after all they had gone through to save Frosty in the beginning.

Another incident involving the farm occurred during a Sunday afternoon dinner. As we sat around the table eating, I noticed out of our sliding glass door that a cow was standing in the middle of the highway. We all flew out of the house and headed for the farm, some on foot and me in the car. We managed to get her back in the corral but then noticed that the bull we had rented was missing. Where could a huge 1,500-pound black bull have disappeared to? I couldn't help but wonder what it would cost us to replace a bull we had lost. A short time later we discovered that the bull had gone visiting over at the neighbors across the road. The owner didn't know where it had come from so he penned it up. Our next problem was how we would get this big animal across the road. We gathered together some willing neighbors and formed a human chain around the bull and escorted him back to the farm. Mission accomplished! What a relief!

I will never forget the Grussendorfs' return home from Montana. We knew approximately when they were due home. One afternoon we saw a travel-all drive up on the edge of the field and immediately we knew it had to be them. After they had been home for a few days, they shared with us how they felt as they arrived closer to home. When they were less than 20 miles from home, they experienced a disappointing feeling rather than one of elation — they almost wished they could turn around and go back to Montana. At that point, I realized how much they loved it out west and knew they had left a part of their heart back there. The months they spent out there away from old friends and family were a time of new growth, new friendships and challenges for their entire family.

I believe there were two main reasons for their return to Minnesota. One was the fact that John had been offered the head coaching position for girls basketball in Esko and this presented a challenge he could not refuse. Secondly, he was experiencing some health problems which he wanted to have checked out. A lot of us wondered if there was a connection between his illness and the tension involved with moving. It was discovered that John was suffering from colitis and it would require some type of surgery. John dreaded the thought of having to wear an external bag so when he heard about a new surgical procedure that eliminated the need for an external bag, he checked it out. We all were relieved when the doctor decided he would be a good candidate for this new surgical procedure. At this point in time we began to feel a great deal of empathy for the Grussendorf family. Mary's role as a wife, partner and helpmate became very apparent as she had to leave her children to be at John's side. The Lord provided the best substitute available in Grandma Aili. She took over and filled in as no one else could. Not only did she run their house and care for the girls but she also was the go-between to relay the reports on John's condition to all concerned (and that was many people). How tired she must have been of talking on the telephone and of the repeated conversations.

John required some follow-up surgery due to a problem with scar tissue. This seemed to go very well. During his recovery from this surgery, Mary decided to come home for a break and to be with the girls. John was doing very well, otherwise Mary wouldn't have left his side. It was during Mary's absence that John began to hemorrhage internally and came very close to dying. Mary was not there during that crisis and I believe that was meant to be for some reason.

John later shared with us that he believed he might die and he asked the Lord to let him see and hold his girls one more time. When he returned home from the hospital after that ordeal, his attitude toward life was very different. He was grateful for each day to be alive and he vowed he would not be a complainer from then on.

The summer of 1982 was a time of recovery for John. He needed a lot of rest. When he started to have frequent black and blue marks on his body, it was recommended that he have a check-up. He went in for complete blood work in August and it was discovered that he had aplastic anemia. We couldn't believe it! Why John? We felt he had been through so much already.

Aplastic anemia sounded like a dreadful disease; even today, some people still think that John has a type of cancer. We wondered how they could treat this disease. In John's case they felt a bone marrow transplant would be the best. The next step was to test John's family members to find a compatible donor. His brother, Tom, was a very good match so he would be the donor. The procedure sounded fairly simple to us; they would remove bone marrow from Tom and inject it into John's body. What we didn't know about were all the side effects John would experience from this procedure. How ignorant we were. John had to have radiation treatments first and then he was placed on many medications as well. All of this combined really took its toll on him. Another factor that had to be very depressing for both John and Mary was seeing all the patients in the ward he was in. Many were young children who had leukemia or some form of cancer. He also came to know others with the same problem he had. Some were doing good; others were not. The future was so uncertain.

John's friends and family back home were very supportive of him in many ways; most importantly, we were upholding him in prayer for healing. I believe that God was in control of the entire situation but when someone close to you is so ill and the time gets so dragged out, you begin to question why and how much longer. It had to be very hard, if not impossible, for John to keep his faith strong at this point. When someone is caught up in the middle of a storm as John was, they need to rely on others' faith to carry them through the storm. It had to be reassuring to him and Mary that many people were carrying them through this storm.

I will never forget what John looked like after the bone marrow transplant. The first time I saw him I was shocked. His color was very gray, he had no hair and his face and cheeks were terribly swollen. He was not a lovely sight and I had to be careful not to show my alarm when seeing him face to face. He was very embarrassed and we tried to put him at ease. He wore a baseball cap a lot to cover his bare head. I remember what a struggle it was for him to eat due to the sores in his mouth and throat. He needed a lot of nourishment to regain his strength and get his weight up but it was very difficult for him to eat. He had to rely mainly on malts for quite some time.

In January of 1983, I had a crisis in my life. My mother had been sick with flu-like symptoms for several days. She refused to see a doctor or go to the hospital. My sister and I took turns staying with her and caring for her. One night I received a call at 2:00 a.m. from my sister. My mother's condition had worsened and she wanted to go to the hospital. My sister wanted me to drive her to the hospital since our car was large and it would be easier for her to ride in. We had freezing drizzle during the night and the streets were like skating rinks. I had to drive so slowly. When I arrived at my parents' home, my dad met me and informed me that they had called an ambulance. It seemed like forever before they arrived. I was chosen to ride along with my mother and when we left in the ambulance, I knew she was in very critical condition and she would be fortunate to even make it to the hospital. I did not panic but I asked God to be in control. I was helpless to do anything else. At the emergency room, we were informed that my mother was critically ill and we should call the members of our family together right away. The next 24 - 48 hours would be crucial.

During those many hours of waiting in the intensive care waiting room, I began to realize a bit more of what John and Mary had been going through. They came to my aid at that time, visiting me, encouraging me and feeding my family while I spent time at the hospital. My mother slowly recovered over a period of several months and our prayers were answered once more.

Our lives were greatly affected by John's illness during basketball season as well. My husband had coached basketball all of our married life and had just retired so he could spend more time with the family. When John Grussendorf realized his illness would take him away from his coaching duties for a period of time, he asked John if he would fill in temporarily. Of course he said yes. We wanted to help out in any way we could. It was probably difficult for the girls on the team to make adjustments with a new coach, but they did, and John discovered he enjoyed working with the girls. As time went on, and John gained his strength back, he started coming to practice but he was not able to take over fully so all three coaches finished out the season. They worked well together.

John's assistant coach, Bob Swanstrom, was an elementary teacher in the Esko School System. Due to cutbacks he lost his teaching job and was forced to get a job elsewhere. His new working hours would not allow him the necessary time schedule that coaching requires so therefore, he had to resign. With this new development, John Grussendorf, the girls on the team and some of the parents put some pressure on John to continue working with the girls basketball program in the role of assistant coach. Since he had enjoyed it so much, and he and John worked well together, he accepted the job. John G. and John B. made up a great team as coaching partners. Their personalities are quite different and therefore, that created a nice balance. John Grussendorf cracks the whip and lays down the law. He really disciplines the girls and they respect him for that. My husband has a great sense of humor and adds a lighter touch to the scene. The two coaches complement one another and they are well liked by all the players.

John's recovery from the bone marrow transplant was a very long, slow process. As time went on, he returned to good health again and we all rejoiced and were very thankful. The biggest change I saw in John was seeing him become more family oriented. In years past, he would frequently go off with "the guys" to fish, play tennis or basketball. Since his health problems, he looks at life differently and spends a great deal more time with his family. They bought a motor home and often will take off for a weekend as a family.

Last winter during basketball season, we had another scare with John. He called my husband at school one day asking him to take over practice that night as he had a doctor's appointment late in the afternoon. During practice that evening, John's brother-in-law came to pick up John's daughters to take them down to the hospital. He told my husband that John was critically ill with a life-threatening pneumonia. We couldn't believe it. John had been fine two days earlier and just seemed to be getting a cold. As we drove to the hospital that night, I prayed. I couldn't understand why John and Mary had to go through another crisis after all they had been through already. My prayer was a plea to God. After all, John had a beautiful family of four girls who still needed their father's guidance. "Lord, you just have to bring him through this *again*." When we arrived at the hospital, all of John's family were there as well as Pastor Hilman. Mary broke down and cried as she told me that John wasn't doing well. I tried to reassure her that God was still in control and we had to keep trusting Him. The doctors had made a diagnosis of septicemia after lab tests were run. We didn't like hearing that word since we had just lost a young teacher and basketball coach from Esko just one month earlier from the same illness and in the same ICU. It would be several hours before the doctors could tell if the medication was helping or not. Those hours really dragged out but during that time I witnessed something beautiful. There was a very special unity as family members and friends showed support to John, Mary and the girls. We also learned that the girls basketball team, their parents, and some church board members were gathered at the church in Esko praying for John's recovery as well.

One of the greatest things about being a born-again believer is experiencing God's love and peace. God has really worked in John and Mary's lives and He will continue to do so. They realize that God has a purpose and plan for them. Someday it will be revealed to us why the Grussendorfs have had so many burdens to bear. One thing is certain, they have touched many lives and will touch even more in the future. They are willing to do the work God has planned for them. Their testimony will be an encouragement to others who face trials and suffering.

Rod Johnson
Esko Boys BB Coach

Many thoughts come to mind when one thinks of the impact John Grussendorf has made on our lives. He exemplifies the following to me:

1. FRIEND — He is always there when you need him, lending a helping hand and an encouraging word.
2. COURAGEOUS — He is not afraid to "walk in the valley of the shadow of death" with confidence in the Almighty.
3. OPTIMISM — He has a very positive attitude on life. He believes in a Lord who has an order to things in this universe. John believes that what happens was meant to be. Do your best and let things come as they may. Face the future with unwavering FAITH.
4. STRENGTH — Nobody could see the pain and agony John has gone through and not

admire the physical and spiritual strength of the man.

5. LOVE — His love for his family, friends, neighbors and mankind in general is remarkable!

In summary, one cannot know John without being infected (pardon the expression) with a love for life. I'm glad he is my friend!

Kerry Juntunen

We were standing by a hole that we had just dug out to plant a small mugho in and discussing how the basketball coaching job had been opened up to him while he was in Montana. He told me about the first meeting that he had with his girls and that he had told his assistant coach at the time to write on the board: *"I HATE COACH GRUSSENDORF."* He went on with the story but I had already drifted off on those words. Yes, I knew him to be intense at times and almost impossibly stubborn at others but I couldn't believe that he would have the foresight to write those words on the board.

I saw it come true, however, as I became an assistant coach in the winter of 1982. He had asked me some time earlier if I would be interested in coaching girls' basketball and every time that I walked by him at church he would say, "I'm counting on you. Don't gum out on me!" I'd smile and say, "Yeah, don't worry, I'll be there."

But when the time for me to "be there" came, he was flat on his back hoping for the best. Practice started under the guidance of Bob Swanstrom and John Bonneville. On the second or third day, a gaunt and wobbly figure came in and sat down at the south end of the gym. I hadn't seen John since he had gotten sick and I swallowed hard and asked for strength when I noticed that he was beckoning me over to him. I smiled weakly and said, "Hey coach — how goes the battle?" He nodded his head slightly and then whispered, "They're loafing out there...Umpierre and Towne should be winning every one of those sprints and look at them...lazy...go get on them! You have to do it because those guys won't." I was surprised but I said, "Sure." I proceeded to give the girls a verbal thrashing. It wasn't long before Eli said between huffs and puffs, "Just because he is here doesn't mean that you have to put on a show..."

I thought about that for a long time. They were used to getting reemed out by him but to have another person come in and try to take his place was insane. He did come back a few weeks later and, armed with a microphone and an office chair, was back at the helm. After a rather lengthy sprint session, I walked down to one end of the gym to grab a loose ball when I noticed Eli in the corner sobbing. "I hate it!" she cried, "I hate it."

Perhaps the prophecy was true.

But over the rest of that year and into the next, I saw something that didn't even closely resemble hate. It was admiration. Admiration and in some cases, even love. John was "the man in the red sweater" (London, Jack, THE CALL OF THE WILD S.S. McClure Co. New York. P.18) and the girls bent under his rule.

I am now a head coach in a small school just 12 miles from where I had first started my coaching career. I have to honestly say that I did not learn a lot about the intricacies of the game, but I did learn something about how to deal with people. I love John for the influence that he had on my life in the short time that I have really known him. But most of all, I love what he stands for . . . like a rock in a swirling sea of compromising positions and half-hearted effort, he stands out.

"I HATE COACH GRUSSENDORF?" Ha, no way!

Quotes from Ball Players

Joyce Diesen

I admire and respect Mr. Grussendorf both as a person and as a coach. During the four years I played for him, he had a lot of health problems and suffered a lot of pain. He pushed himself extremely hard and never complained. In spite of his own problems, he was always there challenging us to do our best. Many times he seemed to over-emphasize the negative by yelling in order to get us to play our best. I feel yelling is good to a point but if it is carried too far, it often does more harm than good. There were times that I didn't like him very much but I wouldn't have traded him for anyone. He was the main reason why basketball was my favorite sport. I'll remember him in the future when troubles come my way and I'll know they can be overcome. His example will always be with me.

Barb Puumala Pearson
(Manager)

John Grussendorf knows what he wants you to do and he won't let up until you get it right. He makes you want to do good for him. He has a good sense of humor and is fun to work for. He taught me to be more responsible by trusting me to do what he asked. He makes you respect him. He was always honest with me — a little hard and too loud sometimes, but I don't think anyone minded. He made me feel needed and important. I brought him gum every day. A lot of good memories!

Marcie Richardson

Coach — you have shown me determination, courage, trust and a special type of love which any true Christian can share. Despite the fact I was kind of the sixth player, your bench buddy, times were frustrating, but all in all you showed me how to be a real fighter. Going the extra mile, no gain without pain and giving 110% will always stick with me.

You fought your way through not only once but three times. I knew you would make it. The level of intensity was sure there for all the players. With your strong faith and all the prayers he pulled. God surely tested you and you just wouldn't give up! I admire your courage and strong faith. May God continue to bless you and your family. You're a living miracle — at least three times over! Love, Hondo.

Debbie Mattinen

John Grussendorf is truly a man of determination and survival, as evidenced in his miraculous healings from his death bed. His story is one of unbelievable trials and answered prayers. I first met Coach Grussendorf as a sophomore in high school. I had heard he was going to be a tough coach but never in my wildest dreams did I imagine how hard he would work us. Through all the hard work and discipline, he got the most out of each girl on the team. He encouraged us to be the best athletes we were capable of being. But above and beyond the many responsibilities of being head coach, he always opened his home and gave of his time whenever there was a need. Through my many phone calls and visits with Coach Grussendorf, I saw another side of this tough coach: his love for the Lord. Being in a coach's position and professing to be a Christian is a very vulnerable position to be in, but Coach

Grussendorf has earned the respect of the team and the community as well. Of course there were times when I felt he stepped out of line, after all he's human too. But he was always willing to hear us out and talk about it. Although it is hard to admit mistakes, he was able to look back and learn and move on. I was always amazed at his trust and faith and that of his wife, Mary. Even through all the physical problems, he seemed to look to the Lord and draw strength and comfort. That is why now we see a man, not of bitterness and confusion, but a man who is strong in faith who has not let go of his determination.

Lori Heikkinen

Looking back at my association with John Grussendorf and my years with the Esko Basketball Program, I can honestly say I would give anything to go through it all over again — the good and the bad.

I'll be the first to admit Coach Grussendorf wasn't always the easiest guy to play for — in fact, there were times in my sophomore year that I was ready to throw in the towel and give it all up. There were times I even cried. Coach definitely fit the description of the word disciplinarian and I had a hard time adjusting to the verbal punishment at first. But one thing he would always say, which I will always remember — the more he yelled at us, the more he loved us. We should start worrying when we didn't hear his voice. I used to often think he must love me a lot!!! After a while, I was able to just take the yelling in stride and by the time I was a senior, although I hate to admit it, I was able to zone him out, especially during games.

Coach Grussendorf is a Christian and he never hid the fact. For that I've always admired and had much respect for the man. It was great to play for someone who didn't just consider us his basketball players —

we knew we were important to him off the court as well as on. We were a family.

Lani Towne

Mr. Grussendorf or simply "Coach" to his players — you loved him, you hated him. But how could you love a man who would yell at you until you felt tears forming in your eyes. A man who would run you until you felt sick. A man who closed his eyes to some people's talents and to other people's shortcomings. Yet, how could you hate a man who pushed you to be your best, on and off the court. A man who was one of the first to call and see how you were doing when you missed a practice because of an injury or illness. A man who would have lost every game of the season if just one of his players found the Lord. He is a teddy bear in a grizzly's disguise. Mr. Grussendorf is the strongest person I know. He's been on his death bed a number of times, yet those who knew him always believed he'd make it again. He was always there when you needed him, treating us all like his daughters off the court. Yet he was so professional, never would get too close to his players. During high school, you couldn't wait to get a different coach, an easier one. But once you got to college, you wished he was right there with you, making you run another killer, another sprint, yelling at you until he was hoarse, punishing you for not having your stocking cap on over your ears. Although Mr. Grussendorf was more than serious about basketball in the winter, in the off season there were a lot of good times . . . going out for ice cream, haying at his farm and having him call the cops on us while camping out in his front yard. Basketball holds some of my fondest memories of high school — thanks to Mr. Grussendorf. We were a family and he was our dad, his wife, like our mom, and his four daughters, like our sisters. I've tried in a nutshell to tell you about this man whom we all love and respect so much. Nowhere are there enough words to give you a true picture of John Grussendorf.

Eli Umpierre

As a coach, Mr. Grussendorf demanded complete dedication to basketball. The first year he coached, my freshman year, he told Lani, Lori and me that we were his to make into the best players we could possibly be. We ran and we ran some more. I had never been so exhausted. Just when I didn't think it was possible to take another step, Mr. Grussendorf would bellow, "Two killers! Go!" We were off and pushing ourselves to our limits. I would drag my aching body to class and people would ask me how come we put ourselves through so much torture day after day. Even if I wasn't all that sure why, I would answer, "Mr. Grussendorf said to." "No pain, no gain." Which is not to say that I enjoyed all the running. In fact, I truly hated it. After seeing how Mr. Grussendorf battled his way through his illnesses and always came out standing, I've seen that a person can have power and endurance to make it through just about anything they may be faced up with. I can honestly say that Mr. Grussendorf has been one of the single biggest influences of my life. Mr. Grussendorf, there are so many more ways that you've influenced my life than those I've written here. I guess some feelings are impossible to be put onto paper. Thank you for everything you have given me. It will last forever. Love, UMP!

Kimberly Juntunen

Although my friendship with John Grussendorf is only five years old, I can remember as a child, riding on the North Cloquet Road past his red barn with the words, "Praise the Lord," painted on it in big white letters. It was an inspiration then and is even a stronger one now. He and his family have helped to paint those words permanently on my heart.

I am out from under the auspices of John's iron coaching-hand but never want to leave the special friendship that has grown between us. As his player for one year, I learned total devotion to the game through my admiration toward him. Despite John's impossible coaching expectations, I worshipped his every command and became dependent on his constant direction. I admit that I was lost in college athletics without his countless demands and on-going motivation.

Oftentimes I thought John's goals were unrealistic and many girls' parents were at the brink of rebellion against this pseudo-god dictator. However, they, like me, saw his strong love and caring for each individual as if they were his own daughter. I have approached him as a father many times for advice and insight. John and his wife, Mary, have brought me through rough times in my faith and family life. They have shared in my joys and understood my pains with an empathy only true friends could show and have given me assistance in my spiritual renewal with God.

Therefore, I question why the Lord has delivered so much pain and suffering to such a mighty servant. It is in His plan, I believe, but what is the reason for it all? At first I thought that God was giving John the opportunity to see his wonderful wife and beautiful girls in a new light so that he could appreciate them more, but he learned that lesson from the first setback. Then I wondered if the Lord was having John look at his own material viewpoint by making him hear his words about living in this world and not of it. I still don't understand why.

I never dreamed that my persistence for a good basketball coach would lead back to the red barn with the big white letters and that I would gain much more than an athletic mentor — I found a true friend! Praise the Lord!

Sam (Kathy) Munter

I have been associated with Coach Grussendorf both as a player and as a part of his coaching staff. First as a player, Coach Grussendorf taught me a lot about dedication, hard work and respect. We all were expected to have these three qualities and if we didn't, we sure learned them awfully fast. He is the type of coach who likes to yell. For the most part, the yelling didn't bother me a bit but there were days I felt like walking off the court. We were his first team so a lot of yelling was necessary to teach us his system. As the seasons have passed, I feel he has mellowed. I learned how to be a "scrapper" — make things happen, hustle, dive and work as hard as possible all the time — practice and games.

As far as respect is concerned, he got the whole team. At first I think it was more fear than respect, but as the season wore on, it was definitely respect. He knew what he was talking about and there was no doubt about it. I learned more about basketball in that one season alone than I had in my previous seasons combined.

As a coach in his system, I gained even more respect for Coach Grussendorf as a coach and a person. I realize now his motives for yelling and being tough on the players and I respect him for having the courage to coach the way he does. He has helped me out tremendously in not only coaching techniques, but also in organizing and running the team. Every time I call with a problem, he is willing to hear me out and decide on a solution. I feel this is the reason his program, elementary up to varsity, is run efficiently and to fit his system. The types of things he wants done, get done because he takes the time to see that they are done.

As a person, he truly amazes me. For all that he has been through, he has never complained or felt sorry for himself. Each new crisis seems to make him even more determined to live and to show others how great it is to be alive. I personally feel that I could call at any time for help and he would be there for me. He is very loyal and will do anything in his power to help me out when I need it. It would be very easy for him to become bitter and full of self-pity, but he instead uses illnesses to show others what God has done for him. He is very clear and open about his dedication to Christ. Each season, he sits the team down and has a talk about the importance of accepting Christ as your personal Saviour and Lord. There is no doubt as to where he stands. I feel this is the most important part of the season. A team prayer is said before each game which is another open commitment of his love for God. Through all his illnesses, he has looked to God for strength and given God the glory for his recovery. This is where I've gotten my greatest respect for Coach Grussendorf. He has made his decision to follow God, sticks by it and lives it. It is evident to anyone who knows him or talks to him.

The best way to summarize my thoughts on Coach Grussendorf is to say that I have grown to love and respect him very much and that he not only has taught me very much about basketball, but also about life and the appreciation of it.

Heidi Helberg

High school basketball definitely brings back many memories for me. When you first started coaching, I was scared to death of you. I really believe that your desire for athletes to do their very best (and pain is gain) is very good, but I couldn't believe how hard you pushed us for just a high school sport. I think your super aggressive attitude made me more and more timid and shy toward you than I have been toward anyone else. You have, however, turned the girls' team around since you've come. When I was in practice, it was really exciting to see improvement, especially if you happened to notice it. When you offered encouragement, it was really meaningful because you only did it if you really meant it. I guess that is why I'd feel so bad when you'd get mad at me for a stupid move or play. I can remember many nights going home feeling like I wasn't worth anything. It also hurt when you'd tell me if I couldn't take the heat to get out of the kitchen. I was very tempted to "get out of the kitchen." I understand though, that was just your way of getting potential out of us.

Having prayer before games was an excellent idea. I think it was a great testimony for you to give us. It was really nice to reflect on the Lord's strength and love before a game.

I know I had some very strong feelings about basketball back then, but that was a few years ago and it really doesn't matter to me anymore. I often remember comments you'd make like being a "blue chip athlete," "pain is gain," "don't be a puppy dog" and so on. Now I use them more for my running than for basketball. I want to thank you for the sincere effort you put into your coaching, even though I have gotten very frustrated with you in the past. I can honestly say that I love you in Christ and I pray that He blesses you with very much happiness in the coming years. I am praying for you and your family and I admire all of you for the faith that has kept you strong in the past couple of years.

Jill Larsen

Through my years in basketball I have grown to

know, love and admire Mr. Grussendorf. As a coach he's like no other I have had and I'm sure he's different from any I will have. He's a dedicated coach in every sense of the word. His rules give you no choice but to eat, sleep and breathe basketball. Even if you could find time to do anything else you probably aren't supposed to do it.

The conditioning is just as outrageous as the rules. It's all something you learn to accept — it's definitely a challenge but it has its rewards. Being involved in his program kind of sets you apart from the rest — it's definitely not for everyone.

Through all the killers, pressure defenses and his non-stop hollering, he pushes his players to their limit — both mental and physical. The worst part is probably the yelling. He has always said, "I'm yelling for you, not at you." For some reason it seemed he was always yelling "for" me. At practice I feel yelling is all right — that's when we should be hollered at. During games though, it should be a little different. The last thing you need when you're playing poorly is someone telling you just that. I think a few more positive comments would be more beneficial than public humiliation.

As a player I tried not to let comments bother me — you learn to ignore them but sometimes that's not so easy. I'm sure he has no idea how many feelings he has hurt (unintentionally) but he has learned now that girls are a little more sensitive or maybe more "emotional" than boys.

I certainly can't say I haven't enjoyed it. I have to admit though that at times I've hated it and maybe even despised him. But there is something about the atmosphere, something about him, that keeps you from quitting. Coach really brings out the best in everyone. No matter how hard he is on you, you know he really cares about you — you're a part of his "family." That's not something you get from any coach. Even though the conditioning, rules and his yelling can be too much at times. I don't feel it's something he should change. As hard as it was, it doesn't compare to anything he has been through. The only fault in his coaching would probably be that he too often overemphasizes the faults of some players while overlooking the faults of others. He doesn't exactly have favorites — but not everyone is treated equally.

Mr. Grussendorf has been an excellent coach but basketball isn't all he has taught me. He's taught me a lot about life and religion as well. Many of the values I have today I have because of him. Through his witnessing and his example, my faith in the Lord has become greater than I ever thought it could be. When I first met Mr. Grussendorf I had many questions about God —it was hard for me to accept something I couldn't see. But through all his trials, Coach never gave up on the Lord. After all the pain he suffered and everything he and his family went through, he still never doubted — and he never forgot God in the good times either. I learned from him the power of prayer, to accept things as they come and to never lose faith in the Lord. I could never explain all the ways he has affected my life —but I hope that I can someday do for someone else what he has done for me.

Sara Mattinen

To start with, I must say you were no ordinary coach. To me you were much more than a coach. You were a disciplinarian, a dad, a friend and also a good example. When I first became a member on your team, I had mixed feelings about you. Being very honest I didn't really care for you as a coach. You made us wear hats, work too hard, you yelled about everything and to top it all off, you told me I was moody and needed to grow up. When I heard that, I thought you were crazy. So my first year on the team was kind of frustrating. The only reason I stayed in it was my love for basketball and every once in awhile you told me I had "potential."

As time went on I started to realize you were a pretty good coach and a very special man. You worked us hard not only to be winners on the court but also in life. You stressed to put up a good fight and to never quit. "When the going gets tough, the tough get going." You not only told us that but you also showed us in your fight for life. You've been a great witness and I'm really thankful to have had you as a coach. God bless you! I love you, Coach!

Stacy Pelletier

Mr. Grussendorf: The best part about having you as a coach was the fact you were so caring and you wanted us to do what you knew we were capable of doing. I'll never forget the game when I was playing really bad and you kept calling me over and telling me different things so that I would play better and the last time you called me over, you bent over and told me you loved me. That was the sweetest thing you could have done for me. That meant a lot to me! Thanks.

About the only thing I had a hard time with was getting yelled at during a game. I mean I probably deserved it, but it made me more nervous and then I played worse. I could handle it at practice but not at the games.

I have learned a lot from you through the years. You're not just a coach — you're a very special friend to me and a lot of other players too. I think you strived for that. You never compromised your belief in anything —always being straight forward and getting right to the point which is what I like best in a person. Even though it seemed you would get upset often, I realized you were frustrated with God and life so I would understand it and not take it personal.

With all your sickness, you still stayed as strong as ever. If you don't know by now, you brought many people closer to God and each other through their praying for you, etc.

You're not a selfish man: God, family and your job were first priority. I was scared of your sharpness but through the years I saw deeper and realized how tender you really are. Even when you called and wanted me to move back and then you realized that it wasn't right for me — you called me back. That meant the whole world to me. I admire you so much for that too.

You are a very special person to me and the best coach I'll ever have. I'm almost sorry I know you so well because that is all the harder to leave. You're always close to my heart. I love you lots!

Medical Glossary
GLOSSARY OF TERMS

Aplastic Anemia — a non-cancerous blood disorder in which the bone marrow is not functioning and therefore not manufacturing blood cells.

Blood Cells:

Red Cells (erythrocytes) — cells that make up the largest portion of your blood and carry oxygen throughout your body

White Cells (leukocytes) — cells that aid in fighting infections and carry antibodies for your immune system

Platelets (thrombocytes) — smallest blood cells; they help your blood clot and stop bleeding

Bone Marrow — liquid in the hollow middle of the bones where your blood cells are made

Chemotherapy — use of drugs to treat disease by either destroying abnormal cells or slowing their growth

Hemotology/Oncology — a division of medicine that focuses on diseases involving the blood and cancer

Hickman Catheter — a soft flexible tube inserted under the skin, used to help provide fluids and drugs to your body and for easy access to your bloodstream for blood drawing

Plebotomy — the process of drawing blood

Radiation — treatment used to prepare your body for transplant by destroying diseased cells and helping to suppress your immune system

Side Effects — possible responses of your body to drugs and radiation. Everyone's responses vary in kind and severity.

Transfusion — a process that supplies your body with

specific kinds of blood cells you may lack until your bone marrow starts making its own. It's most common to receive platelets and red cells. However, white cells may be given for severe infections.

Station 41 is a protective isolation unit designed for both adult and pediatric patients undergoing bone marrow transplants.

Two blood tests are given to both you and your donor. The purpose of these tests is to determine whether you and your donor's white cells match. White cells protect you by fighting off anything foreign that enters your body. Your body would immediately recognize and destroy any white cells that were not exactly like yours. For this reason, it is essential that your donor's white cells match yours.

The first test you and your donor will take is the Human Lymphocyte Antigen (HLA), which examines the characteristics (antigens) of your chromosomes. The second, the Mixed Lymphocyte Culture (MLC), combines your white cells with your donor's to see how they respond. If they do not try to destroy one another, the cells can be used for your transplant.

Once you start chemotherapy, your body's ability to fight against infection is reduced.

Mouth Care — You may get mouth sores from drugs and radiation. They can be painful. It is very important to keep your mouth sores clean to prevent other infections from occurring. Brush your teeth with a very soft brush or soft toothette (plus use salt and soda and not toothpaste).

Chemotherapy refers to any drug used to treat sickness. Drugs are given to you before your bone marrow transplant for the following reasons:

1. To destroy diseased cells (immature white cells or "blasts") in your blood and bone marrow.

2. To destroy your immune system (your body's way of fighting off anything foreign that enters it) so it will not be able to reject the new marrow.

Diseased cells grow rapidly. Chemotherapy is effective against diseased cells because it affects rapidly growing cells, like the diseased ones in your body. However, it can also affect normal fast-growing cells in your body, such as those in your mouth, stomach, intestines, bladder and hair. When this occurs you may experience temporary side effects of hair loss, nausea, vomiting and mouth sores. In fact, side effects are a sign that chemotherapy is actually working.

Cytoxan (Chemotherapy Drug) CTX
Precaution: To help prevent bleeding in the bladder, you will be getting fluids at a fast rate (called a flush) through an IV, starting about eight hours before your first dose of CTX and continuing for at least 24 hours after your last dose. You will need to urinate every hour, day and night, during this time. This will help pass the CTX from your bladder quickly and will prevent irritation to the lining that may cause bleeding.

OKT-3 — Action: Suppresses your immune system and may be used to prevent or treat Graft vs. Host disease.

TRANSPLANTATION

Your donor will go to the operating room and under anesthesia will have bone marrow (a bright red liquid) withdrawn through many needle sticks in his hip bones. The donor is asleep during this procedure which lasts about 2 hours. Before you receive your donor's marrow, some blood may be drawn from you to make room in your bloodstream for the new marrow. This procedure is called a phlebotomy. The bone marrow is given to you through an IV in the same manner that you receive a blood transfusion. The recovery period following the transplant is a time of waiting and *close* observation. Side effects from drugs and radiation may appear. You are most susceptible to bleeding and infections at this time.

Bactrim — given orally twice a day to prevent pneumocystis lung infections.

Mycostatin — given orally every 4 hours to help prevent candida (yeast) infection of the mouth and gastrointestinal tract. For the best effect, it should be swished around the mouth well before swallowing.

Because of chemotherapy and radiation, your blood counts (white cell, red cell and platelet counts) will fall and you may require transfusions until your marrow recovers. These counts will begin to rise once your new marrow "grafts" or "takes." Usually, the white blood cells rise first. Daily blood tests are also done to check the progress of your new marrow.

While your new marrow is taking hold, Graft vs. Host disease becomes a possibility. This occurs when your new bone marrow (the graft) recognizes your body (the host) as foreign and sends out lymphocytes to attack it. Graft vs. Host disease can develop shortly after a "take" of your new bone marrow is seen or up to several months after engraftment.

Three target organs may be affected by Graft vs. Host disease: the skin, the intestinal tract and the liver.

Methotrexate *(MTX)*
Action: to prevent your new bone marrow (graft) from recognizing your body (host) as foreign.

Possible Side Effects:
    1) mouth sores
    2) lowered white count
    3) elevated liver enzyme functions
    4) loss of appetite

Prednisone
Action: to help prevent the new bone marrow (graft) from recognizing your body (host) as foreign.

DISCHARGE

You may leave the hospital when evidence strongly indicates a marrow graft take, your white count is high enough to guard against most bacterial infections and your platelet count is high enough to prevent spontaneous bleeding.

Due to radiation, dry skin is not uncommon. It is a good idea to use bath oil with the bath and an additional lotion as needed to help prevent skin breakdowns.

Preventing Complications: Avoid large groups. It is very important to stay away from people with an infectious disease such as measles, chicken pox, mumps or strep throat.

Leaving for Home

Signs and Symptoms of Infection and/or Graft vs. Host

- a. unusual area of redness or swelling
- b. complaints of pain
- c. rashes or changes in skin color
- d. diarrhea
- e. sore throat
- f. coughing, fast respirations, complaints of shortness of breath
- g. flushing
- h. fever

Three Important Reasons to Notify a Doctor

1. signs and symptoms of Graft vs. Host or infection
2. fever of 101 or greater
3. suspected contact with a person having a contagious disease